Copyright © 2016 by John Smed and Justine Hwang
Artwork by Leah Yin Studio, www.leahyin.com

Published by Prayer Current
106 – 1033 Haro Street
Vancouver, BC V6E 1C8
CANADA

info@prayercurrent.com

All rights reserved.
No part of this publication may be reproduced, stored in
a retrieval system, or transmitted in any form or by any means –
electronic, mechanical, photocopy, recording, or any other –
except for brief quotations in printed reviews, without
the prior permission of the publisher.

WWW.PRAYERCURRENT.COM

WORDS FROM PARTICIPANTS

"I used to avoid talking about Jesus but now I enter conversations with courage and conviction of what to share and how to pray with a seeker."

"If you find evangelism intimidating, then this is for you. You will find an open door to talk to people about God through prayer that is easy to walk through."

"If you love your friends and family, you need to learn to be a 'prayer evangelist.' The greatest need of the human heart is to meet Jesus. I am fired up! I will trust God to open doors for me to offer to pray the Lord's prayer with seeker friends."

"In prayer accountability Jesus opens my heart to rise above my fears and busyness, to see my friends and feel compassion as he does, and to trust him for open doors and boldness in sharing his love."

"When a non-Christian is sharing their challenges with me, I'm not accustomed to asking them if I may pray for them right then. It is already a reach for me to say that I will be praying for them (privately). But after this training, I have gained confidence to practice asking: 'Would you mind if I prayed for you now?' God opened the door to pray with a non-Christian going through a challenging heath trial. I was surprised by her openness and started praying out loud with her. I think she was touched. I now see praying for with and for non-Christians as a tangible expression of showing care and Christ's love with them."

"I have been praying for some people year after year. I never thought about praying with them. It is simple and makes so much sense."

"I have new hope for friends I love and care for."

"I prayed with my brother in the midst of a difficult situation. He thought I would scold him. I just prayed with him. It was wonderful."

"I'm challenged to not take no for an answer when I pray, and to keep on knocking on God's more. I want to engage in spiritual conversation and pray with friends and teach them to pray."

ENGAGE THE CONVERSATION with God, with believers, with seekers

Course Overview: Introduction 6
　　　　　　　　Course Framework: The Sequence of Practical Prayer Skills 7

1. Prayer Evangelism Begins With Enjoying Friendship With Jesus 8

Scripture Study: Growing Deeper In Prayer Friendship With Jesus (John 15:13-18)................9
Skill Training: Preach and Pray The Gospel Into Your Heart 11
Readings: Journey In Prayer Chapter 1: Our Father In Heaven 14
　　　　　　God In The Conversation Chapter 3: A Papa Prays For His Children 16
Bring It Home: Pray It Forward, Share It Outward 18

2. All Effective Prayer Flows From Jesus' Intercession 19

Scripture Study: Grow Deep By Going Deep In Christ's Intercession (Heb. 10:19, Rom. 8:34-35).........20
Skill Training: Pray The Lord's Prayer As The Framework For Intercessory Prayer..............23
　　　　　　　Lord's Prayer Grid Template...24
Readings: Journey In Prayer Chapter 2: Holy Is Your Name 26
Bring It Home: Pray It Forward, Share It Outward 29

3. Friends Bring Friends To Jesus In Prayer 30

Scripture Study: Persevering Prayer For Friends (Luke 11:5-8, Genesis 18) 32
Skill Training: "Oikos" Prayer Map Of Relationships 35
　　　　　　　Pray For The Heart Of Your Seeker Friends..36
Readings: God In The Conversation Chapter 10: When You Haven't Got A Prayer 37
Readings: God In The Conversation Chapter 1: Temple In A Taxi 38
Bring It Home: Pray It Forward, Share It Outward 41

4. We Pray For Christ's Harvest Eyes And Heart 42

Scripture Study: Above All: Jesus Came To Seek And Save The Lost 43
Skill Training: Understanding Biblical Hospitality..45
Readings: Journey In Prayer Chapters 3, God In The Conversation Chapter 4 49
Bring It Home: Pray It Forward, Share It Outward 53

5. We Pray For Open Doors And Jesus' Power To Proclaim 54

Scripture Study: How Paul The Evangelist Prays For Himself...55
Skill Training: Pray For Divine Appointments To Converse Boldly With Seeker Friends 57
Readings: Journey In Prayer Chapters 4 + 5 60
Bring It Home: Pray It Forward, Share It Outward 65

PRAYER EVANGELISM TRAINING FOR MINISTRY LEADERS

6. Team Up With Mission Prayer Partners 66
Scripture Study: Power In United And Persevering Prayer 68
Skill Training: Assess Your Prayer Life With Others 71
Readings: JOURNEY IN PRAYER Chapter 5 72
Bring It Home: Pray It Forward, Share It Outward 75

7. Bring God Into The Conversation With A Seeking Friend 76
Scripture Study: Paul's Creative Evangelism (Acts 16:11-34) 79
Skill Training: Pray For Appointments 82
Readings: JOURNEY IN PRAYER CHAPTER 6: FORGIVE US OUR DEBTS 83
Bring It Home: Pray It Forward, Share It Outward 86

8. Engage In Rich Spiritual Conversation With Seeking Friends 87
Scripture Study: Jesus Dives Deep Into Spiritual Conversation 89
Skill Training: A Modern Day Example 90
Ask Diagnostic And Exploratory Questions To Bridge Prayer And Spirituality 92
Prepare To Share Your "Prayer Testimony" 94
Readings: GOD IN THE CONVERSATION CHAPTER 12: Outwardly Wasting, Inwardly Renewing ... 97
Bring It Home: Pray It Forward, Share It Outward 102

9. Pray With And Teach Seeking Friends How To Pray 103
Scripture Study: Review Of Personal Scriptures 105
Skill Training: Pray Jesus' Kingdom Prayer Applied To Seeker's Common Requests ... 106
GOD IN THE CONVERSATION CHAPTER 11 108
Readings: JOURNEY IN PRAYER Chapter 7: Lead Us Not Into Temptation 112
Bring It Home: Pray It Forward, Share It Outward 114

10. Pray For Harvest Joy And Answers 115
Scripture Study: Jesus' Promise Of Answered Prayer (John 4:36, 14:14, 15:7-8, 16:23, Luke 15:7) ... 117
Skill Training: Evaluation: Key Growth, Answers To Prayer 118
Readings: GOD IN THE CONVERSATION With Everyone 119
Bring It Home: Pray It Forward, Share It Outward 121

How to Stay Engaged 122-123

COURSE OVERVIEW:

Introduction

Everyone wants to make a friend. In the current chaos of communication it is a challenge to get the conversation going. It is hard to keep it up. Face book and other social media provide a posed snapshot of life. We realize this does not satisfy our need for meaningful relationship. We need living face-to-face communication to go deep. We need to listen and speak- again and again- in order to go deep with God and with friends.

This training is about building dynamic prayer friendships. We build and deepen friendships one conversation at a time. This is true of any friendship- with a person or with God. True prayer is a conversation with God.

Praying to God or conversing with a friend is two-way. The best conversations involve careful listening and thoughtful speaking. The best way to converse with God is to first read and listen to his word- reading and meditating on scripture. As you listen to his word, the appropriate responses will arise from your heart. The same is true as you converse with others. First, listen carefully. Seek to understand. Ask good questions. A fitting word will arise.

Our prayers to God are part of our friendship with others. When we pray for someone we bring God into the friendship. When we pray with someone God's presence becomes close and personal. When we help someone pray, we free them to have their own conversation with God. When they know how to pray, they are already on the path to knowing Jesus and becoming his friend.

Praying for and with someone is a part of loving them. Recently, a woman who was learning how to build friendships with prayer, explained how her brother phoned from his home in Europe to say "I am leaving my wife." The line was quiet. He was waiting for her to scold. She didn't. She said, "I know how much you are hurting. Can I pray for you now?" A moment of silence, then "Yes." She prayed a lengthy and grace filled prayer for her brother." God ministered. They grew closer to God and closer to each other.

There is no formula for building a prayer friendship with God or with people. Friendships and the conversations that make up a friendship, have an ebb and flow. We need to navigate our relationships by prayer. Let God open doors and hearts. God will let you know the right time to share a prayer or to share your story.

COURSE FRAMEWORK: The Sequence of Practical Prayer Skills

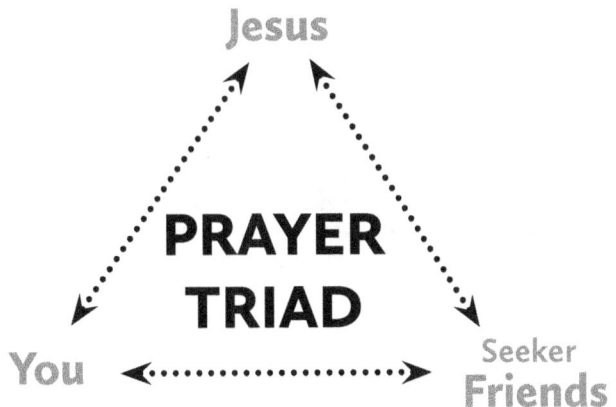

Training Themes → *Week to week practical prayer skills*

PRAYER WITH JESUS

WK 1: Enjoy prayer friendship with Jesus (John 15:13-18)
→ *Preach and pray the gospel into your own heart*

WK 2: All effective prayer flows from Jesus' intercession (Heb. 10:19, Rom. 8:34-35)
→ *Pray the Lord's Prayer as the framework for all intercessory prayer*

WK 3: Friends bring their friends to Jesus in prayer (Luke 11:5-8)

KEY THEME : How are you growing in your prayer friendship with Jesus?

PRAYER FOR YOU + WITH BELIEVERS

WK 4: Pray for harvest eyes and heart (Luke 19)
→ *Pray the gospel to counter your fears and pride*

WK 5: Pray for open doors and power to proclaim (Eph. 1:16-20, Col. 4:2-4, Rom 1:16-20, 15:31)
→ *Pray for divine appointments to share boldly with seeker friends*

WK 6: Team up with mission prayer partners (Eph. 1:19-20, 3:20-21)
→ *Assess and map out your prayer life with others*

KEY THEME : How are you praying with one another for your friends to know Jesus?

PRAYER FOR + WITH SEEKER FRIENDS

WK 7: How to bring God into the conversation (Acts 16:11-34)
→ *Pray for opportunities to dialogue with friends*

WK 8: How to engage in rich spiritual conversation (John 4:7-26)
→ *Prepare to share your prayer testimony*

WK 9: Lead a friend to Jesus by teaching them to pray
→ *Pray the Lord's prayer applied to seekers' needs/requests*

WK 10: Pray for harvest joy and answers (John 4:36, 14:14, 15:7-8, 16:23, Luke 15:7)
→ *Evaluate growth and answers to prayer*

KEY THEME : How are you sharing Jesus in prayer with friends?

WEEK ONE:

Prayer Evangelism begins when you Enjoy your prayer friendship with Jesus

Introduction

Prayer Evangelism begins with our prayer friendship with Jesus. He invites us into a remarkable prayer friendship with him.

> *13 Greater love has no one than this, that someone lay down his life for his friends. 14 You are my friends if you do what I command you. 15 No longer do I call you servants, for the servant does not know what his master is doing; but I have called you friends, for all that I have heard from my Father I have made known to you. 16 You did not choose me, but I chose you and appointed you that you should go and bear fruit and that your fruit should abide, so that whatever you ask the Father in my name, he may give it to you. (John 15:13-16)*

Jesus' declaration of friendship is all the more precious because we live a world where much friendship is increasingly virtual or shallow. Close confidants are on the wane and too many have no close friends at all (see Duke University study). We are a lonely generation.

A friend is someone you can count on. Jesus puts his life on the line for us.

A friend is someone to confide in. Jesus brings us into a two-way friendship communication with him in prayer.

Do you struggle with loneliness? Are you aware of a deep inner need that no one you know can reach? Do you need a good friend? Jesus invites you to be his friend.

Apart from Jesus, we experience a kind of solitary confinement, the isolation and loneliness that characterizes our age.

We enjoy Jesus' friendship in prayer as we dialogue with him. Apart from prayer, friendship with Jesus can never begin or grow. In prayer with Jesus we grow rich in our friendship with him and rich in friendship towards others.

The closer the friend, the more certain he will bring them into his most important plans and purposes. Jesus lets us know what he is doing. He also invites us to be a part of what he is doing through our prayers. Jesus invites us to pray in his purposes, and to bring forth 'fruit-answers.'

> *You did not choose me, but I chose you and appointed you that you should go and bear fruit and that your fruit should abide, so that whatever you ask the Father in my name, he may give it to you. (John 15:16)*

Bearing the fruit of Jesus' friendship means more than making personal requests. We live out his friendship as we intercede on behalf of others. (See week 3).

When Jesus calls us friends, that makes believers friends with each other. Think of children in a loving household. They are fellow playmates who enjoy unrestricted access to the Father. They share in their prayer friendship with God.

For example, the Lord's prayer is a prayer we pray together. It is a family prayer. All the requests are plural: "Our father, give us our daily bread, forgive our trespasses, deliver us from evil." This prayer is most faithfully and fully prayed when we pray it with others. As we do, our friendship with Jesus and each other grows.

ENGAGE THE CONVERSATION with God, with believers, with seekers | WWW.PRAYERCURRENT.COM

Scripture Study

1. Growing deeper in prayer friendship with Jesus

13 Greater love has no one than this, that someone lay down his life for his friends. 14 You are my friends if you do what I command you. No longer do I call you servants, for the servant does not know what his master is doing; but I have called you friends, for all that I have heard from my Father I have made known to you. 16 You did not choose me, but I chose you and appointed you that you should go and bear fruit and that your fruit should abide, so that whatever you ask the Father in my name, he may give it to you. (John 15:13-16)

On your own, read this passage.

Jesus calls you a friend. From this passage write down the different ways Jesus proves his friendship – the different things he does for you.

PRAYER PRACTICE:

Take time to thank him in prayer.

Now read the passage from another point of view. What are the privileges and obligations you have as a friend of Jesus? Write them down.

Think of ways you can be his friend today.

PRAYER PRACTICE:

Pray it through.

2. Now we are able to form prayer friendships with each other

In groups of 3, read John 15:13-16 out loud.

Discuss the different ways we can be prayer friends with each other. Think of similar ways that we are prayer friends with Jesus.

PRAYER PRACTICE:

Pray for each other.

Pray for prayer friendships to multiply in your church, your family, and your ministry.

3. It is in prayer that we grow deeper in our friendship with Jesus

For this reason I bow my knees before the Father, 15 from whom every family in heaven and on earth is named, 16 that according to the riches of his glory he may grant you to be strengthened with power through his Spirit in your inner being, 17 so that Christ may dwell in your hearts through faith—that you, being rooted and grounded in love, 18 may have strength to comprehend with all the saints what is the breadth and length and height and depth, 19 and to know the love of Christ that surpasses knowledge, that you may be filled with all the fullness of God. (Ephesians 3:14-19)

In triads, read the passage out loud.

Discuss how prayer imparts our growth in Jesus love and friendship.

This is an intercessory prayer. Discuss how we also impart Jesus' love to others by praying for them.

PRAYER PRACTICE:

Pray this blessing (Jesus' deep love) into one another!

PREACH AND PRAY THE GOSPEL INTO YOUR OWN HEART

Evangelism isn't just sharing Jesus with seekers. It's for Christians too!

The path of following Jesus is a journey consisting of many moments of re-conversion and trusting him again, deepening in our experience of Jesus, in every area of our lives. We may profess faith in Jesus, but in reality there are times we act independently of him in ways that deny his power and grace. We live as though we need to perform well for God or obey him more in order to receive his acceptance.

"Without [Jesus], we're helpless and hopeless; we seek someone or something else to give us hope and joy; we rely on our own power (or lack thereof) for faith and strength; we fear other things, which can then control our lives. Bottom line, you need to believe the gospel in order to step out and obey Jesus.

You need to believe he has saved you. You are forgiven and loved; there is no record of wrongs against you. You need to believe he is saving you. You can do all things through Christ who gives you strength. You need to believe he will save you. You have nothing to fear because your future is in his hands." (*Saturate Field Guide,* Jeff Vanderstelt and Ben Connelly)

As maturing disciples, we must continually rely on the Holy Spirit to reveal Christ more fully in our hearts, renewing our minds, and transforming our actions and lives in increasing surrender to Jesus and his lordship.

If we are not experiencing intimate friendship with Jesus *ourselves*, we have little to witness about and share afresh with *others* around us. We need to *preach* the Gospel to ourselves and have God give us a fresh revelation of Jesus. A growing prayer friendship and confidence in Jesus' love for us counters our struggles against a Spirit-filled freedom and power to witness and share Christ with others.

We must pray the Gospel into our hearts, especially when we struggle with unbelief, fear, guilt, or shame. Or perhaps when we struggle with pride, relying on our own effort to be good and become holy, or to save ourselves with our own righteousness

We must pray the Gospel into our hearts even when we are spiritually feeling strong, in gratitude and worship to Jesus. We stand firm even then because there is an enemy who will attempt to thwart us when we are in tune with God and seeking to follow Jesus and be used by him.

In either case, the recognition that our own salvation is supernaturally based solidly in Christ's finished work leads us to pray with grace and boldness for God's supernatural transformation in ourselves, and in the lives of those for whom we pray.

Regularly rehearsing preaching the gospel to ourselves also makes us ready to give a reason for the hope we have in Jesus.

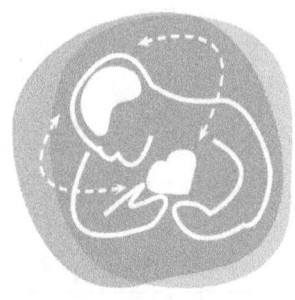

Examples Of Preaching And Praying The Gospel To Yourself

From Independent Orphan to Dependent Child

Thank you Father that you chose to adopt me as your own. You're the perfect Father. Forgive me when I turn away from you and live as an orphan, distrusting your goodness, relying completely on myself. Forgive me when I push others away and hurt them out of fear of being rejected. My sin and independently rebelliously living apart from you doesn't reflect how you live in perfect unity as Father, Son, and Holy Spirit.

Thank you Jesus for leaving the comforts of your heavenly home to come for me. You lived completely dependent on your Father, never breaking relationship with him – until the Father turned away from you and left you all alone because you took my sin on the cross.

You came back to life, conquered death and eternal separation from God to fully restore me to the Father. Empower me to live with abandon in complete trust and dependence on you because you will not abandon me. Fill me with love to live interdependently with others in the family of Christ now and forever.

Freed from the Law to Love

Father, forgive me for relying on my own effort to live a good life, creating my own laws to justify myself. When I keep them, I feel good; when I fail, I feel miserable. This grieves you because I reject Jesus' righteousness. I hurt and shame those around me by subjecting and judging them by my laws. I confess I can't change myself. Trying harder brings frustration. My laws act as a barrier and distance me from you and others.

Thank you Jesus for being the perfect expression of God's law, keeping it perfectly. You didn't deserve death, yet you died in my place, fulfilling God's law on my behalf, paying the sentence and releasing me from the power of sin.

By faith, I now rely on Jesus' perfect record. Thank you that when I feel the weight of your Law, or my own laws condemning me, it leads me back to the cross and to Jesus' righteousness. Change me from the inside out. Fill me with your power, so that I can live freely in relationship with you and with others, without judging myself or them so harshly in light of your grace. Thank you for the freedom now to love others with grace.

Practice "preaching the gospel to yourself"

In what ways do you try to become holy, justifying yourself by your own strength, actions, or discipline? By doing so, where are you placing your hope? What does it look like to rely instead on Jesus' finished work on the cross, to abide in Christ's resurrection power?

Where do you struggle with unbelief, fear, guilt, or shame? What is Jesus' grace and truth and word to you? How is he inviting you to draw near to him?

Drawing from your reflections above, write a prayer "preaching the gospel into your heart." Confess your struggle. Meet Christ there. Ask for him to fill you with his Spirit and resurrection power.

PRAYER PRACTICE

Share with the person next to you.

Pray the gospel into each other's hearts.

Pray for an opportunity to share this current testimony in a spiritual conversation, with a seeker, or a believer.

Readings

OUR FATHER WHO IS IN HEAVEN

Chapter 1 from *Journey in Prayer: Learning how to pray with Jesus*

Prayer is not one-way. It is two-way. Think for a moment of the ways you picture prayer. Is it the penitent reciting the rosary? Is it monks spinning a prayer wheel? Is it the faithful bending low on prayer mats?

Though they may evoke powerful images, ritual incantations and relentless repetition are indications of "one-way" prayer. Prayer is not only about us getting through to God. Prayer is about God getting through to us so that we can discover his fatherly love for us. When we pray "Our Father" we are asking that we might come to know God better.

Our prayers fail if they are just one way. Luther said, "Few words and much meaning is Christian prayer. Many words and little meaning is pagan prayer." The prayer Jesus teaches us is two-way. In two-way communication we look for a reply when we speak, and we come to realize that God is eager to know and enjoy us. As we grow in our comprehension of who God is, we begin to have comfort, freedom and confidence in talking with him. We gain assurance that we are heard by him, and that he will answer and give us what we need.

We are adopted – chosen – by our heavenly Father

Several years ago, friends of mine named Stan and Lori Helm adopted their son Nicholas from Russia. By the time I met him, Nicholas was a beautiful little boy, full of life with curly auburn hair. It was hard to imagine the life he had left behind. The unsanitary orphanage had left him in ill health and covered in sores. He had seldom been held. I said to Stan, "Wow. Nicholas just won the adoption lottery with you and Lori."

Without a blink, Stan replied, "No, John. You're wrong. We won the lottery here. No one in the world could be happier than we are."

His words struck me. It made me think about "sonship" with God. He is our adoptive Father. Could it be that God is just as thrilled as Stan and Lori?

The name "father" gets God's attention

My children are the only ones who use "Dad" when addressing me. In fact it's the only name they use. If one of them calls me "mister" they probably won't get my attention. If I am not watching a hockey game, "Dad" gets through to me every time.

It is the same with God. We can try praying to a "Higher Power," we can meditate on the "Ground of Being," or we can study the "Inner Light." I doubt we will command God's attention with these generic phrases. We get God's full attention when we call him by his favorite name – "Father."

In the same way, when Jesus prays to God he calls Him "Father." Although there are 72 names for God in the Old Testament, and several more in the New Testament, every time Jesus addresses God, he calls him "Father."

Father, I thank you that you hear me always.
Father, I want those you have given me to be with me where I am, and to share my glory.
Father, if it be your will take this cup from me.
Father, forgive them, they know not what they do.
~Gospel of John & Luke

Heavenly adoption made possible

How, then, do we gain the incredible privilege of calling God "Father"?

Simply this: When we trust in Jesus for forgiveness and eternal life, he confers upon us his own Royal Sonship status. By adoption, we become true sons and daughters of God. This means God views us the same as his only Son – along with all the benefits and access to him that Jesus has. In his letter to the Galatian Christians the apostle Paul explains this in dramatic terms:

But when the time had fully come, God sent his son, born of a woman, born under law, to redeem those under the law, that we might receive the full rights of sons. Because you are sons, God sent the Spirit of his Son into our hearts, the Spirit who calls out, "Abba, Father." So you are no longer a slave but a son; and since you are a son, God has made you also an heir. ~Galatians 4:4-7

ENGAGE THE CONVERSATION with God, with believers, with seekers | WWW.PRAYERCURRENT.COM

Not only should this take our breath away, it is the key to all effective prayer. In prayer we now call God "Abba" –an affectionate term a Jewish child uses to say "daddy." We are able to leave behind our orphan aloneness and rest in the eternal "Daddyness" of our God.

What this looks like when it comes to prayer

When you do this, you are able to come to God in freedom. You no longer have to plead your good works to earn your way in. Once you have trusted in Christ, you are God's child and nothing can ever take this from you. As the writer of the book of Hebrews writes,

Let us then approach the throne of grace with confidence, so that we may receive mercy and find grace to help us in our time of need. ~Hebrews 4:16d

When you talk to God, you no longer have to do penance and beat yourself up for your sins. You are forgiven the second you confess. God bears no grudge and remembers no sin. He allows you to leave behind the trappings of religion and put on the full joy of being his child.

I think of our grand-daughter Kaiya. When she comes into our home, she doesn't sit in a corner hiding, waiting for us to notice her. She runs up and simply demands attention. This is her privilege as our grand-daughter. She can ask for anything she wants. We might say no sometimes, but we could never be offended, no matter what she asks.

He is our Father "in heaven"

There are many weak and neglectful fathers in the world. But God, dwelling in the eternal reality of heaven, is the original perfect and changeless Father – "from whom all fatherhood derives." *Ephesians 3:15* He will never abuse, neglect or use you. His love for you will never corrupt or diminish.

When I pray "Our Father" I know I experience the results of having such a perfect Father. I learn to receive and rest in the presence of God – where I belong. I know I can demand his attention. He will never be too busy. I can ask him for anything I need. He will never be offended. He is willing to listen. He is able to answer.

"Our Father" is the first request of this prayer

If it were up to us, we might want to jump right into prayers of confession – just to get rid of a bad conscience. We might start by crying out, "Help Lord! I am drowning here. I need you now!" But Jesus teaches us to bond with God as Father, and if we start solidly with "Our Father," the rest of our prayer will be transformed.

As we pray each request of Jesus' prayer, we keep in mind that we are coming before a kind and generous Father. We ask boldly, because we know he is not offended. Teresa of Avila said, "You pay God a compliment when you ask great things of him." Jesus said, like every good father, your Father in heaven "delights to give good gifts to his children." Confident and effective prayer begins with "Our Father."

We start here. We can go no further until we know him as Father. This precious truth should be carried into all our requests.

Conclusion

Remember Nicholas? Stan and Lori went to Russia one last time to finish the adoption procedure. After finishing the paperwork, Stan stepped into the room and saw Nicholas in his orphan environment. He was covered in scabies – a bright red rash caused by small parasites. He had blisters on the bottom of his feet, the palms of his hands, and all over the inside of his mouth. He reeked. The orphanage did not have money for diapers so he was often left in his own excrement.

With his voice breaking, Stan tells me, "I just wanted to hold him. I wanted to comfort and heal him. But more than anything else, I wanted Nicholas to know just how much Lori and I love him."

What a beautiful picture of God's adoption of us. He sees us in the orphanage of the world. With a breaking heart, he notices the scabies of our discontent, the blisters of our unhappiness, and yes, the stench of the sin we have too long remained in.

Rather than reject, despise and judge us, he embraces us. He heals, cleans, and forgives us in his grace. He adopts us to be his sons and daughters. And he takes us home to live with him forever. Now we call him "Daddy."

A PAPA PRAYS FOR HIS CHILDREN
Chapter 3 from *God in the Conversation*

He is earnest. "How do you pray? How should I pray for my children?"

This young man is Muslim.

Our conversation starts earlier. I am reading a book. We are moving five hundred miles an hour at thirty five thousand feet. Apparently, this heavenward experience frees some people to talk about God.

He is gazing out the window. I notice he is young – so young I'm surprised when he tells me he is married and has two young children.

He glances over and asks what I am reading.

I tell him I am reading a book on prayer. "I want to dive in and go deeper in my prayer life."

He smiles, "I do as well."

He is curious. So am I.

"May I ask you a question? Can you tell me, what the difference is between prayer and meditation?"

He ponders for a moment. "I'm not sure. I know what prayer is but am not sure about meditation. What do you mean by meditation?"

"It seems to me that meditation takes us inside. It's an attempt to connect with one's self. On the other hand, prayer is directed upward and is an attempt to connect with God."

"Yes. I see what you mean. That makes sense."

I ask him, "Do you pray?" "Oh yes, I pray to God every day as part of my religion. It is very important to me."

"Are you Muslim?"

"Yes, I am."

"Do you observe Ramadan?"

"I am not strict in this."

Ramadan is the ninth month of the Muslim year, during which strict fasting is observed from sunrise to sunset. It derives from Arabic Ramadan, 'be hot.' Ramadan can occur in any season; originally it was in one of the hot months.

I ask, "When you pray, what do you ask God for?"

"I pray for my children. I love them deeply. I want to be able to teach them how to live well. I pray they will believe in God and enjoy the life he has given us."

Our conversation turns to parenting and family life. We discuss the challenges of raising children today. His two children are not yet in school. We agree it is a tough time to raise kids. The challenges are real for those who believe in God. How can we help our children understand our beliefs in the current craziness of the internet, social media, advertising, and the avalanche of secular beliefs? It's not easy to guide them into a life of purpose and dignity.

"Yes," the young man says, "This is a very great concern to me. I want my children to have real hope – more than prosperity. I am very concerned about this. I pray about it all the time."

His openness is refreshing.

I tell him, "My wife and I have raised five children. We have grand kids. I understand and very much agree with your concern. I admire your love for your children. I am encouraged to see a father so very prayerful."

At this point an announcement comes over the PA. "We are beginning our descent into Vancouver." He ignores this and continues the conversation.

His eyes are lit with intensity. "Please tell me how you pray. I want to learn how to pray better – especially for my children."

What a great question. What a privilege to be asked.

I take a long minute to think before replying.

"I am pretty sure I pray for the same things you do – for my children and grandchildren. I want them to grow up with faith in God and to live a life of purpose. I don't want them just to be successful so they can have more than others. I pray for them to have a loving heart towards God and towards others."

I add, "There is only one significant difference between my prayer and yours."

"What is that? Please tell me."

"When I pray I always pray in the name of Jesus."

He's not offended. Muslims have a great deal of respect for Jesus. His eyes are wide open. He wants me to continue.

"The Old Testament prophets teach that God is infinitely holy. I know you also believe this. I realize God is holy and I am not. I can never approach God on my own merit. I can't just run into his presence with my prayers.

The problem is deep. No matter how hard I try – no matter how much I pray or how much good I do, I cannot make myself worthy to approach God. One of the prophets speaks these words from God, *"Who would dare of himself to approach me?"* (Jeremiah 30:31)

"I believe Jesus makes it possible for me to pray. He died on the cross to bring me to God. He wins me forgiveness of sins. He invites me to pray. Now I freely come into the presence of God. I trust in Jesus and come in his name."

This young father takes it all in. I'm sure he understands. He is Muslim so I don't need to explain concepts of holiness and forgiveness. He has a far off look. He is going inside – taking time to think this over.

Wheels touch down and we taxi to the gate.

He comes out of his thoughts, and turns to me with a smile, "Thank you. I am very glad we had this conversation. Thank you for sharing these things with me."

"I feel the same way. It has been a blessing to meet you."

I add the Muslim sentiment, "God has meant it to be."

Bring it Home

Pray it forward:

- Pray to grow in enjoying your prayer friendship with Christ.
  Confide with Christ. Share your everyday thoughts, as well as your innermost feelings, fears, and needs with him. Receive his grace, assurance, and intimate friendship.
- Write one "gospel-aha" moments from this week, where you experienced Christ in a fresh way. Pray the gospel into your heart.
- Pray for new prayer friends – so you can be part of a prayer evangelism triad.
- Pray for an opportunity to begin a dynamic prayer friendship with a seeker.

Share it outward

- Share what you are learning about prayer and the gospel with a good friend.

Readings:

- Read ahead and prepare Week 2.

WEEK TWO

All Effective Prayer Flows From Jesus' Intercession

"In intercession our King upon his throne finds his highest glory; in it we find our highest glory too. Through it He continues his saving work, and can do nothing without it; through it alone we do our work, and nothing avails without it…. The power of the church truly to bless rests on intercession – asking and receiving [the Spirit] and heavenly gifts to carry to men." ~Andrew Murray

"In his life Christ is an example showing us how to live. In his death he is a sacrifice satisfying our sins. In his resurrection a conqueror. In his ascension a king in his intercession a high priest." ~Martin Luther

INTRODUCTION

Growing in prayer means growing in Christ's intercession. Our prayer friendship with Jesus flows from his intercessory work on the cross. All of Jesus' prayer for us is formed in the fiery furnace of his loving sacrifice for us.

As our high priest and mediator, Jesus not only forgives our sins, he brings us into his exalted presence. This is once for all. We become residents of heaven, members of the family.

> *Father, I desire that they also, whom you have given me, may be with me where I am, to see my glory that you have given me because you loved me before the foundation of the world. (John 17:24)*

This 'residence' with Christ is determinative in our prayer access to the Father. Servants enter by permission. We do not have to enter through the back door as a servant might. Guests come and go. We do not enter only occasionally as a guest might. We have come through the front door of Christ, who says "I am the door," now and forever, once and for all.

Yes, we reverently approach God in prayer, yet we are not coming from outside to inside. We do not have to ask permission to enter. We are already in! We abide in the home of God, one with Father, Son, and Spirit. We are seated with Christ at the right hand of the Father.

The word the Bible writers use to express this free and open access to God is <parrhesia>. This means 'free and open speech.' It is most often paired with speaking or preaching and is translated as 'confidence,' 'boldness,' 'openness.'

> *Therefore, brothers…we have confidence to enter the holy places by the blood of Jesus. (Hebrews 10:19)*

And again,

> *[14] Since then we have a great high priest who has passed through the heavens, Jesus, the Son of God, let us hold fast our confession. [15] For we do not have a high priest who is unable to sympathize with our weaknesses, but one who in every respect has been tempted as we are, yet without sin. [16] Let us then with confidence draw near to the throne of grace, that we may receive mercy and find grace to help in time of need. (Hebrews 4:14-16)*

Christ intercedes for us at the cross. He continues to intercede for us in heaven, continually and forever. In other words, he always prays for us, based on his finished work on the cross. This removes all doubt and anxiety from our heart:

> [34] *Who is to condemn? Christ Jesus is the one who died—more than that, who was raised—who is at the right hand of God, who indeed is interceding for us.* [5] *Who shall separate us from the love of Christ? (Romans 8:34-35)*

And again,

> *Consequently, he is able to save to the uttermost those who draw near to God through him, since he always lives to make intercession for them. (Hebrews 7:25)*

This means our access to God is won at the cross and our residence with God is maintained by the continual intercession of Christ.

Because of Christ's intercession – and our resulting residence with Christ – we have great confidence that our prayers will be answered.

> *By this we shall know that we are of the truth and reassure our heart before him; for whenever our heart condemns us, God is greater than our heart, and he knows everything. Beloved, if our heart does not condemn us, we have confidence before God; and whatever we ask we receive from him, because we keep his commandments and do what pleases him. (1 John 3:19-22)*

Hans Urs Von Balthasar wrote some important thoughts about prayer. He uses the following encouraging phrases to express what <parrhesia> prayer means:

> *"neither ashamed, nor fearing shame"*

> *"an innate right to be there and to speak"*

> *"the door stands open"*

> *"we do not have to approach him as if he were an aloof monarch"*

Because Christ has once for all brought us into the presence of the Father:

Prayer is how we enjoy our residence with God.

Prayer is how we abide in Christ and grow in our union with him.

Praying together is how we share in our communion with Father, Son, and Spirit.

It follows from Jesus' intercession for us that we learn to intercede with others and for others. We introduce others to the friendship of Jesus when we pray for and with them. (See week 3.)

Growing in prayer means growing in Christ's intercession

On your own:

Live in the intercession of Christ: completed, present, forever

Therefore, brothers...we have confidence to enter the holy places by the blood of Jesus. (Hebrews 10:19)

Reflect: What difference does it make to pray as a resident of heaven rather than a servant or guest.

PRAYER PRACTICE

Enjoy and practice 'resident prayer' for 6 – 10 minutes.

34 Who is to condemn? Christ Jesus is the one who died—more than that, who was raised—who is at the right hand of God, who indeed is interceding for us. 35 Who shall separate us from the love of Christ? (Romans 8:34-35)

How does this passage help you 'preach the gospel to yourself' as you pray?

Write down a few 'prayer doubts' with which you struggle.

PRAYER PRACTICE

Pray 'with' Jesus about these doubts. Use this passage.

THE LORD'S PRAYER AS INTERCESSION

"Our" is the pronoun that makes us pray for others as well as ourselves. This is a family prayer.

⁷ "And when you pray, do not heap up empty phrases as the Gentiles do, for they think that they will be heard for their many words. ⁸ Do not be like them, for your Father knows what you need before you ask him. ⁹ Pray then like this:

"Our Father in heaven, hallowed be your name.
  Your kingdom come,
  Your will be done on earth as it is in heaven.
  Give us this day our daily bread,
  and forgive us our debts, as we also have forgiven our debtors.
  And lead us not into temptation, but deliver us from evil.

¹⁴ For if you forgive others their trespasses, your heavenly Father will also forgive you, ¹⁵ but if you do not forgive others their trespasses, neither will your Father forgive your trespasses.

In groups of three, discuss: What is the difference between 'many words' of pagan prayer – and this prayer of Jesus'?

What does it mean to pray this prayer with Jesus?

What is the heart of each phrase of this prayer? Write down one or two key words that summarize the heart of each line.

Our Father in heaven,

Hallowed be your name.

Your kingdom come,

Your will be done on earth as it is in heaven.

Give us this day our daily bread,

Forgive us our debts, as we also have forgiven our debtors.

And lead us not into temptation, but deliver us from evil.

PRAYER PRACTICE

Pray this prayer together. Have one person pray briefly through one phrase at a time, praying through its meaning and implications. Then move onto the next person who will pray the next phrase. Join Jesus in his intercession with and for others.

Prayer Friendship Skill

PRAY THE LORD'S PRAYER AS A FRAMEWORK FOR INTERCESSION

Some might ask, "Why do we need to learn how to pray? Isn't prayer just talking to God about whatever is on our hearts?" While prayer certainly includes this, the reality is "whatever is on our hearts" is often limited to a narrow self-focus, asking for stress relief from challenges. Even in our intercession for others, it's not uncommon for our prayers to be focused on their survival from the latest difficulties.

You *are* what you pray. You *become* what you pray. Pray in complaint about problems. You become a complainer. Pray thanksgiving and rejoicing in Jesus. You become a grateful, joyful person.

The reality is, many struggle to pray with vision, direction, and purpose – whether it be prayers for ourselves, others, or the world.

As we grow in prayer friendship with Jesus, we can't go wrong in getting to know his heart and talking to him about those priorities. He reveals his heart to us in the prayer he taught his disciples.

The Lord's prayer provides a framework that purposefully directs our prayers to uniquely express his kingdom in our lives and in the world around us. It helps prioritize our intercession from overwhelmed and often shallow prayers – to focused, thoughtful, and deep prayers in light of Jesus' coming kingdom.

The priorities of Jesus' prayer are vast and comprehensive enough to pray through until he comes again!

If you looked at a transcript of every single prayer you prayed, what would it reveal? What kinds and themes of prayers would make up the bulk of your prayers? How would you summarize the heart of your prayers?

How well do your prayers reflect Jesus' priorities in the Lord's prayer?

How often is your prayer for others?

PRAYER GUIDE using The Lord's Prayer as a Template

PATTERN	Day 1	Day 2	Day 3	Day 4	Day 5	Day 6	Day 7
	Our **Father** in heaven	Our Father, **Holy is** your name	Our Father, **Your kingdom** come	Our Father, **Your will** be done	Our Father, Give us this day our **daily bread**	Our Father, **Forgive us** as we forgive our debtors	Our Father, **Lead us** not into temptation, deliver us
PRIORITY	Relationship Drawing close to God	Worship Joyfully Obeying	Proclaiming the kingdom Sharing Jesus	Opening up and trusting God's direction	Thanksgiving Contentment Simplicity	Humility & trust to let go Unity	Commitment to the Kingdom Guidance Advance
Pray God's **PASSIONS** into my own heart							
Pray God's blessing for other **PEOPLE**							
PRAISE for who he is & answers to my prayers							

H ere is a simple sequence of prayer as a way to focus on one priority of the Lord's prayer at a time. Pray through one priority (i.e. one column) from top to bottom at a time. Some like to pray one each day; others prefer to focus on one each week.

1. Upward (PATTERN & PRIORITY)

Start your prayer by focusing on the priority **upward to God**. **Praise** Jesus for the priority. **Meditate** on the priority. Ask the Holy Spirit to show you **what it means.** What does the priority **tell you about God?**

2. Inward (PASSIONS)

Next pray the priority into your heart. Talk with God about it. How is the priority lacking or growing in your heart and life? **What will your life look like** as this priority takes deeper root? Ask Jesus to **transform your heart** and life to be more like his.

3. Outward (PEOPLE)

Now pray for **others** to experience more of God's promises and priority in their lives.

Pray for **the world, the church, and the city**, especially as needs relate to the focus priority at hand.

4. Upward (PRAISE)

End by **praising God** for his blessings and answers to prayer. **Recognize** how God has been present. **Thank him.**

ENGAGE THE CONVERSATION with God, with believers, with seekers | WWW.PRAYERCURRENT.COM

For further elaboration on the seven priorities, or more explanation on using this prayer sequence/grid, please see Seven Days of Prayer with Jesus Small Group Study Guide Edition, by John Smed which can be purchased from www.prayercurrent.com/bookstore

Reminder Row*	Our Father in heaven	Our Father, Holy is your name	Our Father, Your kingdom come	Our Father, Your will be done on earth as it is in heaven	Our Father, Give us this day our daily bread	Our Father, Forgive us our debts as we forgive our debtors	Our Father, Lead us not into temptation, deliver us from evil
Pattern for request							
Priority of prayer	Sonship	Worship	Evangelism City Renewal	Mercy Social Justice	Generosity Contentment	Unity Reconciliation	Guidance Advance
Prayers for **Passions** of my heart (heart affections)							
Prayers for other **People**							
Praise for answers to my prayers							

page 25

Permission is granted to copy and distribute this page for personal use. For an electronic version of the list, please visit www.prayercurrent.com/downloads

Readings

HOLY IS YOUR NAME

Chapter 2 from *Journey in Prayer*

When we begin our prayer with "Our Father" we have communion with the relentless and perfect love of the Father. This love is revealed to us in Jesus, delivered to us by Jesus, and is made ours forever in Jesus. We now call God "Daddy"!

When we pray "Hallowed be your name" we are asking that God's name be held in honor and reverence. We pray to partake in his holiness and practice it in word, thought, and deed.

We seldom pay as much attention to God's holiness as we do to his love. But the Old Testament highlights the holiness of God. The prophet Isaiah calls God the "Holy One of Israel" twenty-seven times! In a "melt-down" vision of God, Isaiah sees and hears heaven's greatest beings, the cherubim, continually crying out:

*And they were calling to one another:
"Holy, holy, holy is the LORD Almighty;
the whole earth is full of his glory."*

~Isaiah 6:3

In Hebrew thought this threefold repetition is significant. God is not holy in a comparative sense, or in a superlative sense. God is holy in a super-superlative sense. While angels and men can participate in God's holiness, he is separate from all creatures in his God-holiness. God's holiness is as rich and complex as his infinite, eternal, and unchangeable being. It is revealed throughout the Bible.

1. Symbols of God's holiness

In the Old Testament there are three prominent symbols for God's holiness. These are precious jewels, blinding light, and intense fire. In one place, the prophet Ezekiel includes all three:

Above the expanse over their heads was what looked like a throne of sapphire, and high above on the throne was a figure like that of a man. I saw that from what appeared to be his waist up he looked like glowing metal, as if full of fire, and that from there down he looked like fire; and brilliant light surrounded him. Like the appearance of a rainbow in the clouds on a rainy day, so was the radiance around him. This was the appearance of the likeness of the glory of the LORD. When I saw it, I fell facedown...~

~Ezekiel 1:26-28

First, precious jewels indicate the purity of God. The Bible says that heaven's streets are paved with pure gold "like clear glass," its gates made of pure pearl, and its massive walls built of diamonds and jasper. This is how God describes the purity and the holiness of his kingdom.

Second, the holy presence of God radiates a brilliant light – a light he has created. Anyone who sees the radiance of his glory gropes in "light blindness." Human retinas are not made for this vision.

The third symbol for God's holiness is a fierce fire that, like Moses and the burning bush, attracts and repels at the same time. In the New Testament, we are encouraged to draw near to God, but to do it "with reverence and awe, because our God is a consuming fire." (*Hebrews 12:29*). His holiness is a burning passion for love, justice, righteousness, and truth. But we are warned that his fire is destructive towards anything unholy. It consumes any form of oppression, hatred, malice, envy, and greed.

When we put these three symbols together – precious jewels, brilliant light, and consuming fire – we are overcome by the beauty and power of God's holiness. To see God is "extreme" religion, an experience that prompts us to fall down in awe and reverence. At the same time to even get a glimpse of God's holiness is to yearn for more.

Longing for holiness

On one hand, God is separate from us because, in an absolute and qualitative sense, he alone is holy in a way we can never be. On the other hand, God calls us to participate in and reflect his holiness.

"Be holy as I am holy." (1 Peter 1:16)

Our first parents, Adam and Eve, were created in innocence and holiness. When they disobeyed God they fell from this perfect state. A world fell with them.

Imagine all humankind hurtling down a mountain road in a bus. The bus is piloted by Adam and Eve. Suddenly, the brakes fail and we slam through a concrete median and plunge down a cliff. Inside is a mangled mess. Everyone is crippled, torn, and scarred by this fall – some worse than others.

This is analogous to our spiritual nature. We are broken in the original fall of mankind.

However, no matter how broken and bruised, we are still irresistibly attracted to the glory and beauty of God's holiness. We hunger for our original fellowship with God. This is a dilemma great enough to fill a world of tragedies. We are like moths drawn to a flame. We are wary of approaching the fire because our wings are flammable. At the same time, we cannot survive or be happy without its light and heat.

Though we yearn to ascend to heaven and become one with God in his holiness, we are not made for the journey. We don't have the right stuff to withstand the supernova brightness or heat of his presence.

We pray to partake in God's holiness

So how can we fulfill our longing to draw near to God's holiness without being consumed?

Isaiah asks the same question:
Who can dwell among the everlasting burnings?
His answer: *He who has clean hands and a pure heart.*

(Isaiah 33:14-16)

The solution to our need for holiness is Jesus. He alone has clean hands and a pure heart. He suffered an innocent death to remove our sin, as a substitute for any who will trust in him. At the moment of true belief, a believer's sin is transferred to his account.

Jesus also transfers to us his innocence. By faith in him God accepts us as holy before him. Now we dare to approach God's holy presence – with boldness!

Therefore since we have a great high priest, who has passed through the heavens, Jesus, the son of God... Let us then with confidence draw near to the throne of grace, that we may receive mercy and find grace to help in time of need. (Hebrews 4:14-16)

Forgiven of sin, covered with Jesus' innocence, our wings are now made of the right stuff! We not only ascend to God's holy presence. We live there continually: *"We are now seated with Christ in heavenly realms."* (Ephesians 2:6)

2. God's holy character revealed in his Ten Commandments

God's holiness is revealed in the Ten Commandments, which show us what our holy Father requires of us and what he forbids.

Commands one to four are about keeping God's name holy. First, we are to worship him alone. Second, we are not to identify him with nature or anything man-made. Third, we are not to represent or misuse his name in any way. Fourth, we are to set aside one day in seven for worship, rest and good works.

Commands five to ten are about honoring God's image in the people he has made. Fifth, we are to honor our parents. Sixth to tenth, we are forbidden to kill, commit adultery, steal, falsely accuse or envy our neighbour. In a positive way we are actively to preserve and protect our neighbor's life, spouse, property, and reputation.

Because each of us is made in God's image, God's holy likeness is in every human being. Every man, woman and child, no matter how broken and bruised by sin, still bears the mark of his image and must be loved and honored for God's sake. Our concern for the name of God results in love and concern for our fellow man.

Jesus Christ reveals God's holiness

Jesus reveals the full glory and holiness of God, in his perfect person and perfect nature. Notice how John the apostle describes Jesus' holy life in the same symbols and language used of God:

We have seen his glory, the glory of the One and Only, who came from the Father, full of grace and truth... For the law was given through Moses; grace and truth came through Jesus Christ. No one has ever seen God, but God the One and Only, who is at the Father's side, has made him known. (John 1:4,5,14,17)

Therefore, it is Jesus who supremely reveals and defines holiness for the believer. Holiness is not just a matter of keeping commandments. Holiness involves following Jesus and becoming like Jesus. As we live in the presence and power of Jesus, we become, as the apostle Peter writes, "partakers in the divine nature." (*2 Peter 1:4*)

The gift of Christ's holiness is like a seed sown into the human heart. In time, through prayer and the Holy Spirit, the seed sprouts, grows, and bears leaves and fruit.

Power for God's help to live holy lives

We are no more able to be holy in our own strength than we are able to escape earth's gravity. In our fallen nature we are too weak. In order to break through the force of gravity a rocket requires an upward thrust of seventeen thousand miles per hour. This requires rocket fuel. To overcome the immense gravity of our weakness and sin we need more than natural power.

We need supernatural power. This is why we ask continually to "be filled with the Holy Spirit." (*Ephesians 5:10*) When we pray "Hallowed be your name" we ask for power. When we do, we will be filled with the courage and strength needed for a life of holiness. This is what happened to the early church, and it will happen again today. Consider this remarkable example from the book of Acts:

When they heard this, they raised their voices together in prayer to God... After they prayed, the place where they were meeting was shaken. And they were all filled with the Holy Spirit and spoke the word of God boldly. All the believers were one in heart and mind. No one claimed that any of his possessions was his own, but they shared everything they had. With great power the apostles continued to testify to the resurrection of the Lord Jesus, and much grace was upon them all. There were no needy persons among them. For from time to time those who owned lands or houses sold them, brought the money from the sales and put it at the apostles' feet, and it was distributed to anyone as he had need. (Acts 4:24,31-35)

This is what it means to follow Jesus. This is what holiness is all about.

Worship God's holiness

When we think of worship we might think only about a Sunday morning church service. However, there are two kinds of worship in the Bible. The first denotes a life of worship. In this sense we are to offer our words, thoughts, and deeds in a daily way to God:

Therefore, I urge you, brothers, in view of God's mercy, to offer your bodies as living sacrifices, holy and pleasing to God – this is your spiritual act of worship. Do not conform any longer to the pattern of this world, but be transformed by the renewing of your mind.

(*Romans 12:-12*)

The second kind of worship is praising, proclaiming, and singing the wonders of God's person and his actions. Like the angels, we are to sing:

Holy, Holy, Holy, is the Lord God Almighty. (Isaiah 6:3)

This is where our prayer ultimately leads and finds its fulfillment – to joyous praise of God.

Bring it Home

Pray it forward:

- Practice filling out a simple Lord's Prayer grid. Pray through 3x (3 columns) this week.
- Pray as a resident. Take bold <parrhasia> steps in asking God for fruit.

Prayer and practice steps with others:

- Find a time to pray the Lord's prayer together with two others in this study.
- As part of a friendly 'listening' conversation, seek to share your current experience learning about prayer with one friend – preferably a non-Christian.

Readings:

- Complete readings.
- Read ahead and prepare Week 3.

WEEK THREE

Jesus' Friends Bring Their Friends To Jesus In Prayer

This week we are at the heart of Building Dynamic Prayer Friendships.

We have experienced the rare and deep joy of a prayer friendship with Jesus. We enjoy prayer confidence, feel prayer freedom, and are going deep 'in the intercession of Jesus.' Our heart for others is being shaped as we start to look out at the 'harvest crowd' – the lost and wandering sinners that Jesus loves and has compassion for.

We are filled to overflowing. Imagine finding a hundred loaves of piping warm bread at your door. You only need two for the day. Do you know what that means? That leaves ninety-eight for you to give away! In the fullness of his prayer friendship, we are ready to become prayer friends for others. We learn the lesson that Jesus praying friends bring their friends to him in prayer:

> *And he said to them, "Which of you who has a friend will go to him at midnight and say to him, 'Friend, lend me three loaves, 6 for a friend of mine has arrived on a journey, and I have nothing to set before him'; 7 and he will answer from within, 'Do not bother me; the door is now shut, and my children are with me in bed. I cannot get up and give you anything'? 8 I tell you, though he will not get up and give him anything because he is his friend, yet because of his impudence he will rise and give him whatever he needs. (Luke 11:5-8)*

The parable is about prayer friendships.

Note there are 3 friends here:
- One... the needy and hungry friend
- Two... the friend with bread to spare
- Three... the friend in between.

You are the friend in between the one in need and the one with plenty.

Our role is to bring our needy friend to the other friend in prayer. We speak on behalf – 'intercede' for this friend when we take his need to the Father.

Jesus says the interceding friend is "impudent". He persists to the point of waking his friends entire family. We must persevere- to come home with the bread. No matter if our friend seems reluctant or busy – we cannot leave our friends hungry and without bread. Jesus is telling us, a good friend will not take no for an answer!

You and I have *many needy friends*. So many are quite helpless and unable to fend for themselves. *There are friends all around us.*

Some friends are Christians – "destitute and afflicted" wandering the mountains of North Syria and around the Middle East. They are martyrs and refugees, homes smashed and looted, relatives murdered. We cannot leave them plundered and beaten by the road- while we walk by the other side. We take them to our great and mighty friends in prayer.

We have many friends, neighbors, relatives, and colleagues who are "without hope and without God in the world." They cannot provide for their own souls. They do not know where to find hope and God. We know the way to hope. We can bring them there in prayer!

There are examples of this kind of prayer friendship in the Bible. Remarkable among them is the narrative of Genesis 18 which depicts Abraham interceding not only for his nephew Lot, but also for an entire city.

Like Jesus followers, Abraham is called a 'friend of God'. James 2:23

God appears as 3 angels. He comes to visit Abraham and enjoys a meal with him. He confides in Abraham that his wife Sarah will soon be pregnant and have a promised child.

Next God lets Abraham know why he has come. An outcry has come to heaven from the oppressed widows, orphans and poor in the city of Sodom. God has come to 'hold court' and if it is true God will judge the wicked.

In the name of friendship, God chooses to confide with Abraham:

> *The Lord said, "Shall I hide from Abraham what I am about to do,*
> *see that Abraham will surely become a great and mighty nation*
> *and all the nations of the earth shall be blessed in him?" (vs. 17,18)*

Abraham understands this revelation as an invitation to pray for the city. He stands in between his friend God and the needy city of Sodom. Abraham stood before the Lord...Abraham drew near and said, "Will you sweep away the righteous with the wicked?... What if there are fifty righteous in the city. Will you not spare the city for the sake of the fifty righteous?... Far be it from you! Shall not the God of all the earth do what is just?

A prolonged interchange ensues, where Abraham negotiates with God, "What if there are forty righteous?.... thirty ... twenty...ten?" God listens to Abraham and hears his prayer. God will spare the city if there are only ten righteous.

This remarkable interchange and prayer of Abraham for Sodom perfectly illustrates Jesus parable about the privilege and power of prayer for those who are called friends of God. Jesus confides in his friends and then invites them to pray for others, so that "whatever you ask the Father in my name, he may give it to you." John 15:16

As friends of Jesus we can be bold in prayer. We can intercede for those who do not know God and know we are heard. Nothing pleases God more than when his friends 'stand in the gap' and pray for lost and needy friends. He wants us to persist until he gives what we need for others.

God loves to answer the prayers of his friends. The Father has bread in plenty to spare. He gives the Holy Spirit to those who ask. He gives gifts and healing. He grants forgiveness and salvation to transgressors. Best of all, for us he is the friend of those who ask.

 *Scripture Study*

Persevering prayer for friends (Luke 11:5-8)

5 And he said to them, "Which of you who has a friend will go to him at midnight and say to him, 'Friend, lend me three loaves, 6 for a friend of mine has arrived on a journey, and I have nothing to set before him'; 7 and he will answer from within, 'Do not bother me; the door is now shut, and my children are with me in bed. I cannot get up and give you anything'? 8 I tell you, though he will not get up and give him anything because he is his friend, yet because of his impudence he will rise and give him whatever he needs. (Luke 11:5-8)

Discuss in Triads. Describe how people are hungry and without bread today.

Think of one or two friends you care about and share about their need for bread.

PRAYER PRACTICE

Pray for each other's friends.

'Do not bother me; the door is now shut, and my children are with me in bed. I cannot get up and give you anything.'

On your own ask:

Why does the friend who has bread to spare turn his friend away?

Does God sometimes or often seem to turn you away as you pray? How do you know if this is the case?

ENGAGE THE CONVERSATION with God, with believers, with seekers | WWW.PRAYERCURRENT.COM

PRAYER PRACTICE

Practice 'impudent' and persistent prayer for some one who is suffering. Think of Christians or people group amongst the persecuted church.

Now practice persistent 'knocking' on behalf of someone you love who does not know the Lord.

What if there are fifty righteous in the city. Will you now spare the city for the sake of the 50 righteous?

In Triads discuss: Abraham prays for a city... and for the righteous in the city.

How can we pray in the same way for the city we live in?

PRAYER PRACTICE

Pray together for your city.

Prayer Friendship Skill

Who is the friend you should pray for?

The New Testament word 'oikos' can help us. Our oikos refers to our local, regional and even global world that we are to pray for. Because we are Jesus friends there is a time and place to pray for those close to us and a time and place to pray for the city nation and world.

Abraham, the friend of God, prays on behalf of a city.

Moses speaks with God 'as a friend' (Exodus 33:11). He repeatedly prays on behalf of the nation of Israel.

We are also able to pray for our nation. It is because so few intercede that our land is in its present troubles:

And I sought for a man that should stand in the gap before me for the land, that I should not destroy it; but I found none.
(Ezekiel 22:30)

God tells us to persist and pray for the worldwide church: "Take no rest and give him no rest until he establishes Jerusalem a praise in all the earth".
(Isaiah 62:7)

Jesus is our intercessor and he always prays for every believer (Hebrews 7:25).

In other words, because we are God's friends, because we have the Holy Spirit to give us love for others and power in prayer, because we pray in the name of Jesus, we are assured that God will hear and answer us.

As we mature in our prayer friendship with Christ we will be able to enter into the larger world of prayer with confidence and power. We need to pray on our own, but joining with others is the best way to experience this power of prayer.

For example, each year during 30 days of Ramadan, the month of fasting for Muslims, millions of Christians have been praying for Muslims around the world to know Christ. This started in the early 1990s. Since the early 1990s millions of Muslims have come to Christ. This is the power of prayer friendship!

Prayer Friendship Skill

EXERCISE: Pray and sketch out your oikos map

1. INNER CIRCLE
Who are you 'closest to'
EG. Family, church, close friends

2. MIDDLE CIRCLE *"Regular Contact"*
Who are those around you that you have regular contact with?
EG. Neighbours, colleagues, fellow students

3. THE GREATER CIRCLE
Praying for city nation and world
Especially refugees, new immigrants, international students, elderly, widows, orphans, poor.

1 INNER CIRCLE: Family, church, close friends

2 REGULAR CONTACT: Neighbours, colleagues, fellow students

3 GREATER CIRCLE: City/nation/world, refugees, immigrants, international students, elderly, widows, orphans, poor.

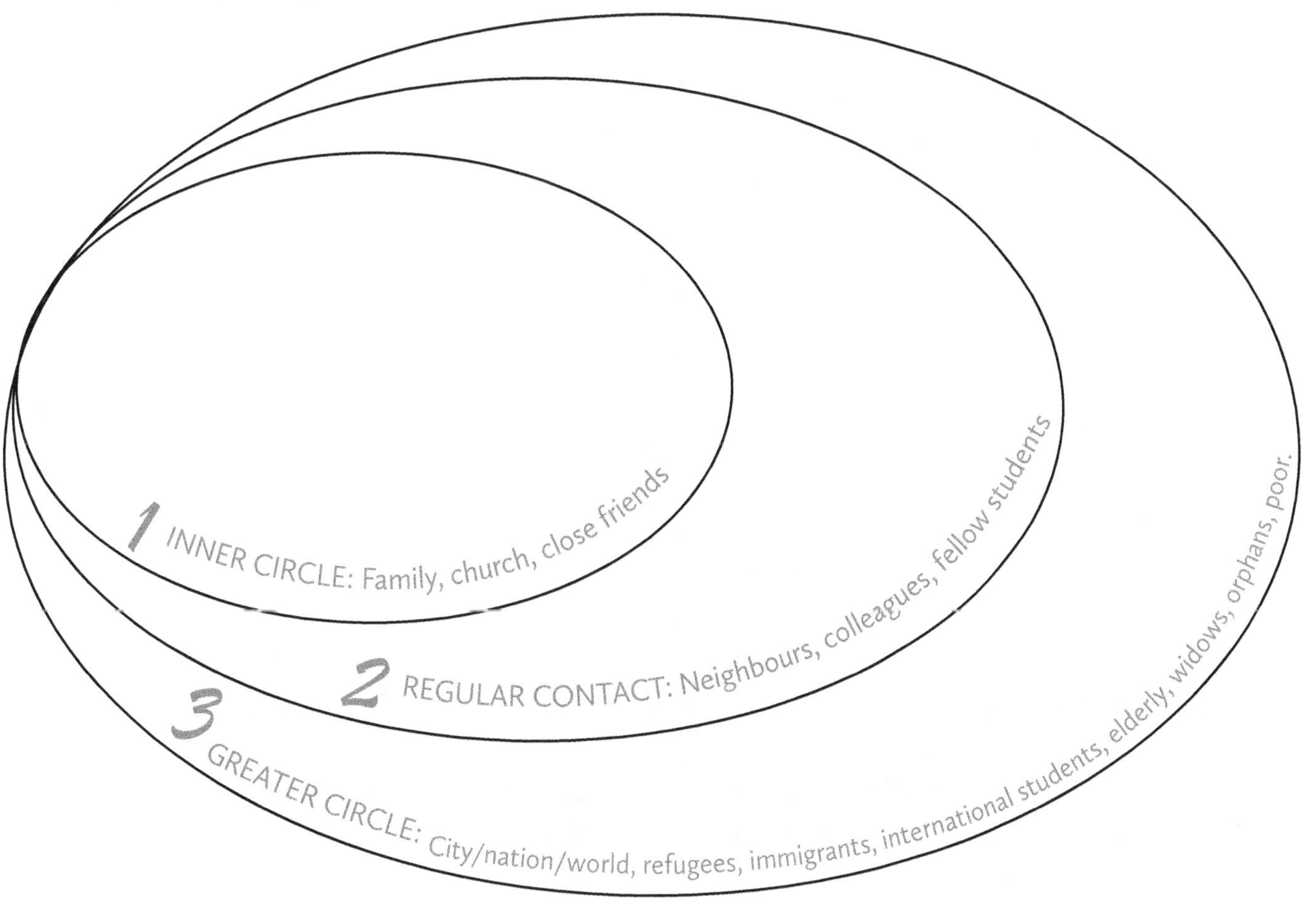

DISCOVER YOUR PRAYER <OIKOS>

Use this framework to pray for one person or group in each Oikos circle.

OIKOS Definition:
- *A house you live in*
- *The inmates of a house, all the persons forming one family, a household*
- *The family of God, of the Christian Church, of the church of the Old and New Testaments*

BEAUTY: What does Jesus (and you) LOVE about them?

BROKENNESS: What makes Jesus (and you) SAD to weep for them?

BROKENNESS: What IDOLS and SINS enslave them?

SO WHAT? How can we respond by PRAYER + HOSPITALITY?

PRAYER PRACTICE

In triads (groups of 3), pray with and for each other's friends.

Praise Jesus for his love for them. Thank him for their strengths.

Confess for and cry out for their brokenness. Pray for Christ to stir and meet their deepest need.

Pray for wisdom and compassion in knowing and loving them well.

ENGAGE THE CONVERSATION with God, with believers, with seekers | WWW.PRAYERCURRENT.COM

Readings

WHEN YOU HAVEN'T GOT A PRAYER
Chapter 10 from *God in the Conversation*

I am in town for a few days to visit my mother and other family members. My mother informs me, "Karl is in a bad way. His cancer is winning and he probably doesn't have long to live." Karl was a good friend of my father, before dad passed away. Mom suggests, "Why don't you drop by and visit him?"

Next morning I go by the hospital. I walk into the room. Family surrounds Karl. They would like to have words. They want to be strong. They just don't know what to say. "Hi John," they greet me politely, but with little enthusiasm. Karl's four grown sons look down, awkward in the situation. These boys are used to being strong but now they are cowed. No one is in charge when death is in the room.

Karl's wife doesn't know what to say either. She whispers, "Please don't upset him."

I turn to look at Karl. He is curled up on the bed. His head is swollen twice its normal size. He appears comatose and is heavily sedated. Karl is in the last stages of brain cancer. I don't think his family has ever been in a room with a dying person before – much less their father.

I'm a friend of the family so they're open to my visit. Still, I am pretty sure they don't want me to talk about God, death, and the afterlife. At the same time, studies show that many of those near death want the truth out in the open. Prayer and discussions about God are usually welcome – if the one sharing is gentle and has some wisdom.

I turn to Karl's wife and say, "Okay. But you don't mind me praying for him do you?" She nods, "That would be okay."

I edge over to the side of the bed and sit on a chair. I face Karl, opposite his swollen face. His eyes are closed. I'm not sure he can hear me.

I take his hand. I begin to pray a simple prayer. I speak slowly and deliberately. It goes something like this...

"Father, I don't know if Karl can hear me, but I know you can speak to him. You know Karl. I pray that he would know peace at this time and that you would give him courage in this battle. You forgive us for asking. We do ask for your kind mercy. You are the good shepherd. You guide us through the darkest valley. Teach us to trust in your might and care. We do not need to fear when you are with us. I pray you would give Karl strength in both body and soul. Give him faith and courage to trust you at this time – to know your strength and hope."

In the middle of my prayer I notice something. It's Karl. He's definitely squeezing my hand. His eyes are closed. He can't speak but he is responding the only way he can – through touch.

I am stirred by this. I'm sure Karl wants me to continue.

"Father, you know each of us intimately and personally. You made us for yourself and our hearts find rest only in you. You are quick to forgive and hear our prayers. Please hear Karl's inner prayer in his very difficult and dark time. Help him to give you all his sorrow and pain. Hold him in your hand. Though we walk through the shadow of death you are with us. Outwardly we are wasting away, but inwardly we are being renewed. I pray that by your amazing grace in Christ that you will renew his inner being. Give him hope and faith, and comfort in his suffering."

Karl's grip doesn't lessen. If anything it grows stronger. His pressure is firm and his hand is warm. I open my eyes for a minute. I see a tear coming down Karl's bloated face. This is heart warming and heart rending...beautiful.

Karl is not given to crying. A burly man, for years he has been a no nonsense construction manager – not sentimental in the least. Still, right now, listening to my prayer, Karl is weeping.

I take heart. I glance up for a brief second. The family look okay. I continue, only now my prayer goes deeper. "Father, I thank you that nothing can separate us from your love. It doesn't matter what the obstacle or pain is, you can carry us through. You give hope and eternal life to anyone who trusts in you. You forgive all our failings when we ask you to. You are the resurrection and the life. There is no sickness that is stronger than you. You heal both body and soul. Please help us to believe in you – and to trust you in this dark and difficult time. Strengthen Karl, I pray. Give him faith. Help him to trust you. Give him courage and hope that can never be taken away. I ask for these things in the name of your only son, who willingly gave himself us – and gives forgiveness and eternal life to all who ask. I pray this for Karl. Amen."

Karl is still holding my hand as I finish this prayer. When I say, "Amen" he gives my hand a firm squeeze before letting go. His eyes are still wet.

I sit still for a minute. No one says anything. No one has too. It has been transcendent to say the least. I think we all feel something or Someone in the room.

Eventually I stand up. I say my goodbyes. As I walk down the hospital corridor, I feel warm with gratitude. I am immersed in thankfulness. My time of prayer with Karl has not been an accident. God meant it to be. God had something to say to a child he loves. He sent me to pray with him. It is God's way and I am glad.

I know when I pray for Karl I invite God into the conversation. When I pray, I become part of God's conversation with Karl.

I tell myself, "I hope to meet Karl in heaven one day."

He dies a few days later.

A TEMPLE IN A TAXI
Chapter 1 from God in the Conversation

We arrive at Winnipeg International Airport. We are headed to a conference. It's the middle of winter – early morning and bitterly cold. Winter and cold are synonymous in Winnipeg. Affectionately referred to as 'Winterpeg' – this place is known for 'nine months winter and three months tough sleddin.'" We stand in line waiting for a taxi. In sixty seconds, fingers numb. When high wind speed and very low temperatures merge news bulletins warn people to stay home. I mean, 'baby, it's cold outside.'

The line is short. A cab pulls up and we dive in. The cab is toasty warm. We settle in for the thirty minute ride to the hotel and convention center.

The driver wears a turban – so I know he is Sikh. Spot a taxi pretty much anywhere in Canada and there is a good chance you'll have a Sikh driver. They hail from the Punjab province of India. I've experienced their cheerful friendliness on numerous occasions. You get in a cab and they make you feel welcome. Call it hospitality.

They love Canada and are proud of their new country. Canada seems to have an open door policy for their immigration. They adopt our sports with the same enthusiasm they adopt our country. They make rabid hockey fans.

I find it easy to strike up a conversation with Sikh people – especially about prayer. They seem to love discussing their religion.

Most devout Sikhs go to the temple each morning if they can, but some will tune into satellite.

Once we are seated, settled and warm, we exchange greetings. "Good morning, Sirs." He asks if we had a nice trip. I ask if business is good.

A few minutes later I bring up a topic of common interest. We are off and running.

"Do you mind me asking, 'Are you Sikh?'"

"Yes, I am sir."

"So did you have a chance to say your prayers this morning?"

Cheerfully he replies, "Yes. I said my prayers at six. I do so each day."

"Did you go to temple or did you listen to satellite?"

"Oh, I go to temple each morning before work. I also go at the end of the day."

Prayer is at the heart of Sikh worship.

***

Sikhism is true to its eastern origins. It is pantheistic but combines this with monotheistic ideas. Sikhs worship Ultimate reality as one, yet they speak of the creator and address this ultimate reality in a personal way.

They have a deep reverence for their teachers – gurus. They try to be understanding of other religions. Counter to Hinduism, they worship God in abstract form, and don't use images or statues to help them. Sikh worship can be public or private. Sikhs can pray at any time and any place.

The Sikh code of conduct lays down a stern discipline for the start of the day. There are set prayers in the morning, evening, and before going to sleep. A Sikh aims to get up early, bathe, and then start the day by meditating on God.

For the Sikh believer, God is beyond description. They feel able to pray to God as a person and a friend who cares for them. Many Sikhs regard prayer as a way of spending time in company with God.

True to their eastern roots, for prayer to be really effective a person tries to empty himself of everything of this world so that he or she can perceive God.

Although Sikhs can worship on their own, they see congregational worship as having its own special merits. They believe that God is visible in the Sikh congregation or Sangat, and that God is pleased by the act of serving the Sangat.

Congregational Sikh worship takes place in a place called a Gurdwara – a word combining 'guru' or teacher and 'dwara' meaning gateway. At the Gurdwara, through prayer the worshipper connects with the Guru Granth Sahib or most sacred scriptures of Sikhism.

An interesting note – Sikh public worship can be led by any Sikh, male or female, who is competent to do so. This might explains why Sikh women are often strong leaders and freely contribute to any discussion. One commentator elaborates:

"The role of women in Sikhism is outlined in the Sikh scriptures. A woman is to be regarded as equal to the man. In Sikhism, women are considered to have the same souls as men and an equal right to grow spiritually. They are allowed to lead religious congregations, take part in the Akhand Path (the continuous recitation of the Holy Scriptures), perform Kirtan (congregational singing of hymns), work as a Granthi, and participate in all religious, cultural, social, and secular activities. As such, Sikhism was among the first major world religions to imply that women are equal to men. "Guru Nanak proclaimed the equality of men and women, and both he and the gurus that succeeded him allowed women to take a full part in all the activities of Sikh worship and practice."

***

Our taxi host is more than willing to continue the conversation. I can't recall a cold reply when I bring up the topic of prayer with someone who wears a turban. This is a stereotype, but a good one, and true to my experience.

One time my wife and I are visiting New York City. We take a cab. We are halfway into the city and in the middle of a good conversation. I find out our driver goes to temple each day.

"Why do you say your prayers each day?" I ask.

He glances and points to the right. He asks, "Do you see these people?" We are headed down the east side of Central Park. The sidewalk is crowded.

"Yes. I do."

Animated, he says, "If I did not say my prayers, I do not see anyone. When I pray I see people."

I'm impressed. "Wow! Now that's a good answer – and a good reason to pray."

***

Back to the cold morning in Winnipeg. Connan pipes in. "I am a Christian and prayer is important to me as well." He adds, "I love to pray each day wherever I am - and to speak with God at the beginning and the end of my day."

Our driver says, "Yes. This is a good thing."

"In fact, I can say my prayers here and now in this taxi because God is here too."

He agrees, "God is everywhere."

While they're talking a new insight hits me. Call it a revelation. I put what the driver is saying and what Connan is saying together – and come up with a third idea.

I speak up. "Praying anywhere is wonderful. May I tell you something even more amazing? This may surprise you."

I pause for a few seconds. I am still processing my insight. New discoveries take time to form. Revelations need to be savored before we speak them.

"I just realized something as you two were talking about prayer."

Connan turns to look at me. Our host looks in the rear view mirror.

I come out and say it. "I do not have to go to temple to pray. I am a temple!"

In the mirror I see a quizzical look, as if to ask, "What do you mean?"

"I believe God is in me and that I am in God. I am always in the place of prayer because I am always in the presence of God. The Bible tells us that if we believe in God's son, Jesus, we become a temple of prayer for God."

***

This 'temple-within' idea is birthed from a rich complex of scripture. The Bible teaches that Jesus resides in the heart of anyone who puts their faith in him: In John 17 Jesus prays, and asks the father,

> "...that they may all be one, just as you, Father, are in me, and I in you, that they also may be in us, ...I in them and you in me, that they may become perfectly one,...Father, I desire that they also, whom you have given me, may be with me where I am, to see my glory."

Getting to know God is like entering a banquet hall with him as host and the believer as permanent guest:

> "Behold, I stand at the door and knock. If anyone hears my voice and opens the door, I will come in to him and eat with him, and he with me." (Revelation 3:7)

Union with Christ is the essence of the Christian faith – *"Christ in you, the hope of glory."* (Colossians 1:27) This makes each believer a temple – who is always in the presence of God. *"Or do you not know that your body is a temple of the Holy Spirit within you, whom you have from God?"* (1 Corinthians 6:19)

***

I try to explain several ideas in a few sentences. "I can always pray anywhere, anytime because, like every believer I always have access to God. I am always in the presence of God! He actually says that I am a temple of the Spirit of God."

I am not sure how our driver receives this idea. I know I am excited. It takes my breath away.

We pull up to the hotel. It's around the corner from the convention center, only a few steps through bitter cold.

Smiles all around, we are thankful for the ride – and even more thankful for the warm conversation. Our driver has been a gracious host. He has given of himself. He has shared what most matters to him.

This conversation has been special. Because of a real interest in each other's experience of prayer – I learn something new and important about my own prayers.

I come to realize, "I am a temple in a taxi."

Prayer Practice

In groups of three, pray with and for each other's friends.

Praise Jesus for his love for them. Thank him for their strengths.

Confess for and cry out for their brokenness. Pray for Christ to stir and meet their deepest need.

Pray for wisdom and compassion in knowing and loving them well.

Bring it Home

Pray it forward

Pray for God to help you identify specific people or groups in each <oikos> field that he wants you to persist in prayer for... Place and highlight these names. Bring them to Christ in prayer

Personal prayer at home:

- Identify 3 people in each your <oikos> relational field to pray for. Ask: How can I pray to know their hearts?

Share it outward

Prayer and practice steps with others:

- Meet with two others (in person or by phone or online) to pray for these seeker friends.
- Reach out to meet one of your 3 seeker friends (for a coffee, recreation, phone conversation, etc.)
- Ask questions to know them beyond the surface. Practice being present, and listening for where God is already speaking to them

Readings:

- Read ahead and prepare Week 4.

WEEK FOUR

Pray for Jesus' Harvest Eyes and Heart

4

Jesus came to seek and save the lost.

What does it mean to be lost? Jesus teaches us real life in a real life encounter.

That Jesus makes friends with sinners seemed preposterous to the religious elite of his day. When Jesus goes to dine with a tax collector names Zacchaeus, we read:

> *They all grumbled, "He has gone to be the guest of a man who is a sinner."*

Jesus answers this bitter accusation (and defends Zacchaeus, and all his sinner friends) with a strong summary of his life purpose:

> *The Son of Man came to seek and save the lost.*

In Jesus' day, sinners were despised. Nowadays we have a different problem. Now it seems preposterous to call anyone a sinner. "Sinner?" people think to themselves, "Surely things are not that bad. We all make mistakes but isn't calling it sin an exaggeration?"

Recall good King David – robed in royal finery and dispensing justice to his people. He committed adultery and premeditated murder of a loyal servant. Read his confession in Psalm 51.

> *My sin is ever before me. Against you and against you only have I sinned and done what is evil in your sight.*

Explore your own soul with honesty and humility and you will find David's prayer applies to our own hearts too.

Make no mistake about it – the same Jesus who befriends sinners, is the same Jesus that knows we are sinners. In his own words he paints the grim reality of the human heart:

> *For from within, out of the heart of man, come evil thoughts, sexual immorality, theft, murder, adultery, 22 coveting, wickedness, deceit, sensuality, envy, slander, pride, foolishness. 23 All these evil things come from within. (Mark 7)*

Jesus does not mince words. He knows that Zacchaeus is a sinner. Yet Zacchaeus is his friend. Jesus truly is a friend of sinners!

With this dim assessment of our sin, and the glorious truth of his friendship, we still have to ask, "Why does Jesus befriend sinners?" Surely he makes a bad choice of friends.

By examining Jesus' own life and teaching we find the wonderful answer to this question. Jesus looks at people and sees their misery as well as their sin:

> *He had compassion for them, because they were harassed and helpless, like sheep without a shepherd. (Matthew 9)*

Jesus is like a good shepherd. He has a tender and longing heart towards his sheep. He knows them by name, and looks for them when they stray.

ENGAGE THE CONVERSATION with God, with believers, with seekers | WWW.PRAYERCURRENT.COM

When a sheep is lost it wanders from the shepherd and the fold. It is aimless, with no clue to the way home. This sheep gets confused, turning this way and that, hoping to be found by the shepherd.

It finds a path but it leads to the edge of a cliff. It is helplessly stuck, facing a dangerous fall. There is a great precipice below. There is no room to turn around.

Predators abound. A wandering sheep is an easy meal. Apart from rescue, death is immanent. You can be sure this sheep is filled with fear, and experiences the foreboding of danger and death.

The good news is the shepherd has already left the flock. From the moment the sheep strays, he begins his search. He calls out their name. The Son of Man comes to seek and save the lost.

What happens to sheep illustrates what happens to a lost sinner. He wanders in a spiritual wilderness. He has no clue how to get home to safety. He can find no rest. All relentless search for pleasure or power results in an empty weariness. Despair sets in. He or she experiences thirst of soul and misery of heart. Before long this sinner comes to a dead end, with nowhere to turn, he is easy prey for the enemy of his soul. He knows death is around the corner. This death is not just a nameless non-existence. It is a day of reckoning. God has written the law and its consequences on the lost person's heart. They live under the summons of God and anticipate a fearful judgment for wrongs committed. (Romans 2:1) They live under the oppressive shadow of God's retribution:

> *Whoever believes in the Son has eternal life; whoever does not obey the Son shall not see life, but the wrath of God remains on him.* (John 3:36)

I recall conversations and prayers with a gentle young man who strayed into the wrong circles. One day he was cornered. He received a summons to appear before a judge in two months time. The charges were serious – possessing marijuana for the purpose of trafficking. He was guilty as charged. The penalty would be severe. Imagine how he felt during each of those sixty days between the summons and the court date. He could never put it out of his mind. Every waking moment he lived under a summons and an anticipation of judgment. We prayed for him and with him. He seemed repentant.

A lost sinner is someone that is aimless. The greatest sorrow of his life is to be without God. He is missing to God and missing to himself. The greatest burden of his life is to live with a guilty conscience. He is filled with a sense of his own doom.

It is at this moment, and this desperate situation, that Jesus comes to find the lost. He comes to make a friend of this sinner. He does not come pointing a finger. He is filled with pity and compassion. What relief! What a friend of sinners! What a joy to become his friend.

The lost sinner's part is simple. He must accept Jesus offer of friendship. He must admit that he is lost and confess his sin. When he embraces Jesus by faith alone, he becomes his forever friend.

If you have been found, you are a still a sinner – but you are not lost. You a friend of Jesus. He knows you by name.

Your part is also simple too.

Now, like Jesus, you are called to leave the safe confines of the fold, to seek and find the lost. You pray for the lost. In Jesus' name, in the tender compassion of Christ, you make friends of sinners. You extend Jesus' offer of friendship.

Scripture Study

Luke 19: *The son of Man came to seek and save the lost.*

On your own:
In your own words, describe what it means to be lost.

Meditate on your own experience of being lost. Where were you before you encountered the transforming power of Christ? Who would you be today if not for the saving grace of Christ?

PRAYER PRACTICE
Pray to Jesus. Now pray with thanksgiving. Thank him for finding and rescuing when you were lost.

Harvest Prayer (Matthew 9:35-38)

> *And Jesus went throughout all the cities and villages, teaching in their synagogues and proclaiming the gospel of the kingdom and healing every disease and every affliction.* ^{36} *When he saw the crowds, he had compassion for them, because they were harassed and helpless, like sheep without a shepherd.* ^{37} *Then he said to his disciples, "The harvest is plentiful, but the laborers are few;* ^{38} *therefore pray earnestly to the Lord of the harvest to send out laborers into his harvest."*

In Triads, read the passage aloud.
Discuss: What does Jesus see when he looks at the crowd?

What do you see when looking at the crowds?

How can we get 'harvest eyes'?

PRAYER PRACTICE
- Pray to the Lord of the Harvest! Meditate on his heart and what he feels and sees when looking at the people in your life and city.
- Pray for a harvest heart, and for labourers to sent out!
- Pray for opportunities to meet someone who is marginalized, lonely, or needy (international student, refugee, homeless, underemployed, etc.).

Do you not say, 'There are yet four months, then comes the harvest'? Look, I tell you, lift up your eyes, and see that the fields are white for harvest. [36] Already the one who reaps is receiving wages and gathering fruit for eternal life, so that sower and reaper may rejoice together. [37] For here the saying holds true, 'One sows and another reaps.'

In Triads, discuss: Are the fields white for harvest today? If so, what are signs?

Describe the joy Jesus is talking about.

What does it mean to sow? To reap? Share you experience sowing or reaping.

PRAYER PRACTICE
Pray for harvest joy!

UNDERSTANDING BIBLICAL HOSPITALITY: <PHILXENOS>

Apart from God's grace we tend to zenophobia- a fear of strangers. Christ died so that we can learn to love the one who is strange and different from us. <philozenos> means 'hospitality' -the love of strangers. Christian gatherings become places of hospitality. There should be no lonely people in a church.

> *"And the foreigners who join themselves to the Lord,*
> *to minister to him, to love the name of the Lord, and to be his servants,*
> *these I will bring to my holy mountain, and make them joyful in my house of prayer;*
> *their burnt offerings and their sacrifices will be accepted on my altar;*
> **for my house shall be called a house of prayer for all peoples." (Isaiah 56:6,7)**

The church is a guest house:

My house shall be a house of prayer for all nations...

Note that God's house is to be a place of prayer. Note that God's house is a guest home – to receive the outsider. Praying together is a powerful way to build fellowship and friendship- and to welcome outsiders into the community. Instant bonds can be formed in prayer.

A good measure of the health of a church is "how wide is the front door. Is there room for stranger? the poor? the hurting? the difference? "

When I first became a Christian I experienced God's radical hospitality. I was invited to be a guest in a community in the Swiss Alps call 'Labri.' It means 'shelter.' It was a place of safety and honest inquiry. They had several guest houses. The people who lived in the homes did not own them. They were hosts. They welcomed, fed, and counseled any and all who came. Guests were of every kind and from all over the world.

Hospitality is the entire process of inviting and receiving others – those who are outside – into God's house.

Abraham extends aggressive hospitality to 'strangers from another land' pass by his tent:

> *And the LORD appeared to him by the oaks of Mamre, as he sat at the door of his tent in the heat of the day. ² He lifted up his eyes and looked, and behold, three men were standing in front of him. When he saw them, he ran from the tent door to meet them and bowed himself to the earth ³ and said, "O Lord, if I have found favor in your sight, do not pass by your servant. ⁴ Let a little water be brought, and wash your feet, and rest yourselves under the tree, ⁵ while I bring a morsel of bread, that you may refresh yourselves, and after that you may pass on—since you have come to your servant." So they said, "Do as you have said."⁶ And Abraham went quickly into the tent to Sarah and said, "Quick! Three seahs of fine flour! Knead it, and make cakes." ⁷ And Abraham ran to the herd and took a calf, tender and good, and gave it to a young man, who prepared it quickly. ⁸ Then he took curds and milk and the calf that he had prepared, and set it before them. And he stood by them under the tree while they ate. (Genesis 18:1-7)*

The divine identity of these guests was not known to Abraham at the time:

> *Do not neglect to show hospitality to strangers, for thereby some have entertained angels unawares. (Hebrews 13:2)*

Showing hospitality is not an elective. **Welcoming the outsider is constitutive of who God's people are.**

When Christ encounters the buyers and sellers at the temple, he is furious with the lack of hospitality :

> *And he entered the temple and began to drive out those who sold and those who bought in the temple, and he overturned the tables of the money-changers and the seats of those who sold pigeons. ⁱ⁶ And he would not allow anyone to carry anything through the temple. ⁱ⁷ And he was teaching them and saying to them, "Is it not written, that My house shall be called a house of prayer for all the nations'? But eyou have made it a den of robbers. (Mark 11:15-18)*

Note first that Jesus is furious – literally filled with wrath – that God's people were occupying the entrance space dedicated to those outsiders who want to pray and find God. Their first introduction to God would be a commercial transaction!

Also note, once the temple is cleansed Jesus welcomes and heals the blind lame into the temple precincts. He reveals the true nature of God's hospitality.

We each begin as guests in the house of God. God's invitation to each one of us is his supreme hospitality. He invites us into his home and promises to reside in our hearts:

> *Behold, I stand at the door and knock. If anyone hears my voice and* opens *the door, I* will come *in to him and* eat with him, *and* he with me. (Revelation 3:20)

Once the guest becomes a part of the household, he assumes the role of greeter, server, and host in the name of the owner of the house.

No one is to be excluded from God's hospitality. Jesus has broken down the barriers between all nations, all socio-economic classes, between male and female:

> *Remember that you were at that time separated from Christ, alienated from the commonwealth of Israel and strangers to the covenants of promise, having no hope and without God in the world. ¹³ But now in Christ Jesus you who once were far off have been brought near by the blood of Christ. ¹⁴ For he himself is our peace, who has made us both one and has broken down in his flesh the dividing wall of hostility ¹⁵ by abolishing the law of commandments expressed inordinances, that he might create in himself one new man in place of the two, so making peace, ¹⁶ and might reconcile us both to God in one body through the cross, thereby killing the hostility. (Ephesians 2)*

In the world of that time, people were identified by their ethnic origin. Cities were (and still are) divided into various walled areas for each tribe. A new community formed in each city when Christ was being made known. Now people were not called "Jew" or "Gentile" or "Roman" or "Syrian" – they were called "Christians." They did not belong to any of the walled ghettos. Slave, free, Jew, Gentile, poor, rich, in one welcoming community!

Now that Jesus has broken down the wall, now we don't wait for people to come to us. We are to climb over the rubble and bring people in.

Note that the cost of God's hospitality is dear. Jesus removes the dividing wall in his body on a cross. How much should we spend to be hospitable? There can be no limit to the cost of our hospitality because there is no limit to the price paid by Christ to bring us into his house.

God is throwing a great banquet for all nations and he will have a full house. If we do not want to come, he will bring in others. If we do not want to declare his invitation to the party, he will find others:

> *And the master said to the servant, 'Go out to the highways and hedges and compel people to come in, that my house may be filled. (Luke 14)*

The host of the feast is indiscriminate who comes to his party. By the highways and byways were the riff-raff of life – the socially undesirable, the displaced, the neglected, the poor lame and homeless, including the refugees and immigrants among them.

God is not only indiscriminate about his guest; we see in Jesus that he has a preference for the least, the outcast, the poor, blind, and lame, the widow, orphan, and foreigner.

On your own, think of others who need <philozenos>

- In your world, think write down names of those neighbors, friends, family, colleagues, fellow students who need a friend, a prayer, acts of kindness.

How can you team up in your church, family, ministry group to cross the rubble to find others:

- The refugees and immigrants, foreign students who are filling our cities. (Regardless of color or religion or language, God issues his invitation to them)
- Single parents and their children.
- The elderly widow and widower.
- The lonely, homeless, outcast, unpopular, poor people who sit by the wayside.
- The mentally hurting, anxiety laden victims of our chaotic world.
- Anyone who is in need and open to hearing and receiving God's invitation.

Who does your heart feel more of a burden for?

PRAYER PRACTICE

Pray for opportunities to meet someone who is marginalized, lonely, or needy (international student, refugee, homeless, underemployed, etc.). Pray for connections in the city that might open up new friendships. Begin to pray for them.

Readings

YOUR KINGDOM COME

Chapter 3 from *Journey in Prayer*

The Bible's concept of kingdom is rich but not complicated. In its simplest sense, when Jesus tells us to pray "Your kingdom come," he emphasizes that we are to live our lives in light of his triumphant return which will happen at the end of the world. No present suffering, discouragement, or opposition can overcome our confident hope that Jesus will soon restore all things.

But Jesus' kingdom does not come all at once. It comes in stages.

First, Jesus is our "Forever King." As part of the Trinity, Jesus has always ruled and reigned with the Father and Holy Spirit.

Second, when Jesus lived and died for us, he became our "Redeemer King." His death is an inauguration and his resurrection is a coronation. In Paul's letter to the Philippian Christians, Paul writes:

God exalted him to the highest place and has given him the name that is above every name, that at the name of Jesus every knee should bow, in heaven and on earth and under the earth, and every tongue confess that Jesus Christ is Lord.

(Philippians 2:8-11)

Third, Jesus is our "Coming King," the one who will judge and recreate all things at the end of the world. He promises that he will return, vindicate his faithful followers and reveal the injustice of those who reject him:

They will see the Son of Man coming on the clouds of the sky, with power and great glory. And he will send his angels with a loud trumpet call, and they will gather his elect from the four winds, from one end of the heavens to the other.

(Matthew 24:30,31)

Jesus' kingdom is coming in a final sense because he is coming again to renew the entire creation and to bring in the new age.

When we pray "Your kingdom come," we pray as loyal subjects who acknowledge his eternal creator-lordship. We pray as those who accept his saving work in his incarnation. We cry out in eager expectation of his coming again to renew all things.

A modern day metaphor

Living in a western democracy, we may find it difficult to relate to the concept of living in a kingdom. But consider for a moment a modern parallel. Imagine a Fortune 500 company taking over a smaller company that has fallen on hard times.

The buyer is Dominion Realty, a national corporation with offices and operations all over the country. Dominion buys out Independent Realty, a smaller outfit. The day after the takeover, the Dominion boss forms a transition team with these instructions, "You have three years to make Independent into a Dominion company. I do not want to chop this company up. I want to renew and rebuild it. Win over as many employees and managers as possible. And call me any time you need me."

Dominion and Independent may be in similar lines of work, but they have different cultures. Dominion is about team work. Independent values individual accomplishments above everything. At Independent, the philosophy is "pull your weight or you're dead weight." Dominion is concerned about company culture. Independent is concerned about the bottom line.

The transition team arrives on site and gets to know Independent.

After a month of careful listening, they gather everyone together to make an announcement.

Corinne, the spokesperson, starts by stating the situation in simple terms, "We are going to have a Dominion company. Nothing can stop that. But don't think for a minute we want to get rid of you! We want to win you over. Dominion is a great company with a great boss. If you are willing to get on board you can be part of a fantastic future. If not, you will probably quit before we have to let you go." She finishes, "Bottom line, the boss is coming soon. Our only job is to get ready for his coming."

Getting ready for the return of the King

Jesus is the Dominion boss. This world, insofar

as it does not acknowledge his present lordship, is "Independent." The time between his first and second coming is the three-year transition.

Christians are the transition management team. This second coming is unstoppable. It is our job to arrange everything to prepare for that coming and to win people over for our coming king.

During this interim period, we not only announce Jesus coming, we teach, carry out and model the plans of our coming king. Someone said, "Christians are building show homes. Their job is to show what the new neighborhood will look like."

Let's return to our illustration.

At the outset, there are some who want nothing to do with the Dominion takeover. The Independent boss does not take long to make his views known:

"Everything we have worked so hard for is being ruined!"

Before long, he quits, sets up a competitor company and takes some Independent staff with him.

However, other Independent employees are willing to take a look at Dominion. Most lived on long hours and low wages. They were constantly concerned about job security.

The Dominion team wants to reverse this trend. Peter, who is on the transition team, comes up to Jim, an account manager for Independent.

"Jim, I notice you let Frank go last week. Why? He seemed to be working hard."

Jim answers, "Yeah, he tried. But he couldn't cut it."

Peter reflects for a minute.

"Jim, I want you to give Frank another chance. Let's get him some training if he needs it. He seems to have a good attitude. I think we can make progress."

"Okay. You're the boss."

"Actually I'm not. I just work for him – like you!"

"And by the way, Jim, I notice you let six or seven others go in the past six months. I wonder if we shouldn't ask them back, too."

Eyebrows raised, Jim stares at Peter.

He asks, "I don't get it. What kind of company wants to keep everyone on payroll and even hire people back?"

Peter just smiles. He can see things from Jim's perspective.

"I understand. You see, it's our boss. He likes to rebuild things. He likes to make winners out of losers."

He continues, "When our boss was younger, he suffered a personal catastrophe. Everyone thought he was finished. No one gave him a chance.

"But somehow, he came back. It happened suddenly – you might say miraculously. That's why he always gives a second chance."

Jim listens. "Interesting. But what about you?"

"I'm glad you ask. I was a workaholic, so bad that I lost my wife and my kids. Even my business went under.

"I was a useless wreck when, out of nowhere one day, the boss called me. He asked if I wanted to do some transition work. He thought I might be good at it. Now I get to help other shipwrecks like myself. And it feels good – really worthwhile."

"Okay, that makes some sense. But what about the others on your team? What's their story?"

"Pretty much similar to mine. Corinne was forced to quit a high-paying job for a fast-food joint after leaving her abusive husband. Phil has terminal cancer. The boss offered him this job as a way to finish life on a high note. And here he is. Going out in a blaze of glory!"

Jim thought he saw tears welling up in Peter's eyes.

"You see, Jim, this is not just a job. Frankly, I love the boss. He could ask me to shovel manure and I would – in a minute!"

Jim didn't say anything.

He didn't know what to say.

Sharing our story

Taking our cue from Peter, we can understand a little more about Jesus' coming kingdom. Sharing what Jesus has done for us is not just a job. It's about loyalty to our coming king. While we wait for his return we share our story. We explain to others how Jesus has established the kingdom of God once and for all.

We explain that God owns every last atom, proton, and electron in the universe. He is the creator-king and every man, woman, and child owes him worship and thanks. He is the all-powerful king of all kings.

Then I heard every creature in heaven and on earth and under the earth and on the sea, and all that is in them, singing: "To him who sits on the throne, and to the Lamb be praise and honor and glory and power, for ever and ever!"

(Revelations 5:13)

Some Christians feel that talking about the end of the world seems foreboding – even frightening. However, we need to remember this "ending" is a great beginning. All the history of this world is only a brief introduction, merely the cover of a book.

We haven't even gotten to the good stuff yet. In the rest of the story, sorrow, sickness, tears and death will be left behind. What is weak becomes strong. Small fragments of precious faith are refined and perfected. Best of all, anyone who wants to start fresh and to live forever in unimaginable bliss is welcome to become a part of his new world. We – redeemed, but still sinners – get to humbly pass out the invitations!

Living out the values of the kingdom

But there is more to the kingdom than sharing the story with others. We also ask for his grace and Spirit to live out the values and character of his coming kingdom today. We look for our present world to change as a result of his kingdom coming into our lives.

Remember what the boss says, "I want a Dominion company when I come back."

Dominion does not come in to end the doing of business! It comes, instead, to end the way business is done.

This is true of Jesus' transition team, too. Though we have a new king, we live in the same communities, go to the same schools, and work in the same marketplace. We know "down and outers." We know "up and outers." We know "way-outers" too.

We are tasked with bringing the joy of God's kingdom to them, today. When we pray "Your kingdom come," we daily apply our prayers to the deep needs of our cities.

An example in Vancouver

In our city of Vancouver, Lorne Epp directs More than a Roof ministry. It works with local and civic leaders to help the impoverished and mentally ill by giving them the dignity of their own place to live.

Lorne came into this line of ministry after his family had to help one of its own members who struggled with mental illness. It took everything this family had to keep this loved one off of the streets. Jesus used this time to prepare Lorne for helping others in similar circumstances. More than a Roof now serves hundreds of those struggling with mental illness or recovering from addictions. All are welcome. All are given the dignity of a home to live in.

Lorne puts it this way, "Christians need to remember the great commandment as well as the great commission. Jesus taught us to love our neighbor as well as to lead him to faith." The theme verse of Lorne's life is:

Is it not to share your food with the hungry and to provide the poor wanderer with shelter – when you see the naked, to clothe him...Your people will rebuild the ancient ruins and will raise the age old foundations; you will be called Repairer of Broken Walls, Restorer of Streets with Dwellings.

(Isaiah 58:6,7,12)

The outcome of genuine faith, and a genuine desire to see God's kingdom come, will always be a life of kindness, justice, and good works.

Illustrating the role of prayer in preparing for his coming kingdom

Back to our story.

Jim from accounting is almost ready to join Dominion for good. He has one more important question to ask. He walks up to Peter and asks, "Tell me. Where do you get your energy and resolve to keep going? Frankly, I want some."

Peter smiles. "Jim, each of us has a direct line to the boss. If you want you can have one too. He tells each of us to call him day or night for any reason whatsoever. He always answers. And he never seems in a rush. I can't remember him ever ending the conversation. When I have to say 'goodbye,' he says 'Okay, but call back soon.'"

Like Peter, God's children have a direct line, too.

It is prayer. We have unlimited personal and direct access to our father for his friendship, strength and wisdom. There is no obstacle that we cannot face with him at our side. There is no challenge we cannot overcome by his grace and presence through prayer.

Postscript

At the end of three years the boss comes back. Unannounced, he enters from the back. It is pretty obvious who he is.

Everyone has been waiting for this day. As he goes through the offices he starts to smile. He has a feel for things, and things feel good. Peter, Corrine, Ted and Phil look excited and a bit nervous at the same time. Jim feels weak at the knees.

He gathers them together and, with a deep and genuine smile, says, "I like what I see. It feels like a Dominion company. I am really happy each of you is here. You are becoming a real team."

He turns to face Corrine and the other leaders. "Corrine, Peter, Ted, Phil – you have done it again! Good work. It's been a blast hasn't it?"

He turns and looks at Jim, "Oh, and you Jim. From the day I bought Independent I knew you were going to be a part of us. Welcome home."

He adds, "I want you to introduce share options for every employee. I want them to get a share of our success. This location is yours to run for me. Enjoy it. You have already proven you will do a great job."

I hope the point is clear. The greatest joy of believers will be to see the face of Jesus when he comes in his glory. There will be no mistaking him in that day. We will be eager and anxious for him to give his verdict on our work. When we pray "Your kingdom come," we pray to be ready for that day. We ask to hear,

Well done good and faithful servant. You have been faithful with a few things; I will put you in charge of many things. Come and share your master's happiness. (Matthew 25:23)

 *Bring it Home*

Pray It Forward:

Personal prayer at home:

- What are the fears or obstacles that you struggle most with in engaging with non-Christians? (eg. bad experiences, fear of rejection/offending/losing friendship, inadequacy, doubt/unbelief, guilt, coldness of heart, etc.)

- Preach and pray the gospel into your heart to specifically address your struggles. Spend time focusing on Jesus' heart for the lost and his passion and power to bring the lost sheep back into the fold.

Share It Outward

- **Prayer and practice steps with others:**
    - Meet with two others (in person or by phone or online). Pray the Lord's prayer. Pray for your 'oikos' (Week 3) and for your 'philxenos.'
    - Seek an opportunity to encourage a marginalized/lonely/needy neighbour by showing them kind hospitality (and seek to continue the relationship).
    - Share with one of your friends you are praying for. Open a God conversation. Ask them how they feel about talking with you about spirituality, purpose, or God. Explore and bring up Jesus in the conversation. See what they think and feel about him. Tell them what it *felt* like for you to be lost. Share *your experience of joy* in being found.

Readings:

- Read ahead and prepare Week 5.

WEEK FIVE — Pray for Open Doors and Jesus' Power to Proclaim

The heart of leading a friend to Jesus is to pray for them. We gain great momentum when we join with others to pray for our lost and seeking friends.

However, the messenger must also pray for himself – to be in constant communion with Christ – to enjoy him in order to share his love and power with others.

> *"The soul winner must be a master of the art of prayer. You cannot bring souls to God if you go not to God yourself. You must get your battle-ax, and your weapons of war, from the armory of sacred communication with Christ. If you are much alone with Jesus, you will catch His Spirit; you will be fired with the flame that burned in His breast, and consumed His life. You will weep with the tears that fell upon Jerusalem when He saw it perishing; and if you cannot speak so eloquently as He did, yet shall there be about what you say somewhat of the same power which in Him thrilled the hearts and awoke the consciences of men."*
>
> ~Charles Spurgeon, The Soul Winner

We also need the prayers of others in order to be faithful and effective witnesses. We need to build a team of praying friends that we can pray for and that will be faithful in prayer for us.

The apostle Paul writes to praying friends and asks prayer for himself as a missionary. He asks often. The scripture study below surveys his requests.

Paul does not make long and elaborate requests for those he is sharing the gospel with. Instead he asks prayer for the messenger. He knows that God sends and empowers his messengers to boldly, openly, and courageously preach the Word.

Paul asks for three things – for boldness, open doors, and deliverance from evil.

We can use Paul's requests in our prayers, as we pray for each other and to encourage others pray for us. This is kingdom prayer for ourselves.

Scripture Study

PAUL'S KINGDOM PRAYER FOR HIMSELF

Notice Paul prays for three things:

1. Open Doors
2. Boldness
3. Deliverance

Eph. 6:19, 20 ...and for me that words may be given to me that I may open my mouth boldly to make known the mystery of the gospel, for which I am an ambassador in chains: that in it I may speak boldly as I should.

Phil. 1:19-22...Through your prayer and the supply of the Spirit of Christ, according to my earnest expectation, that in nothing I shall be ashamed, but that with all boldness, as always, so now also Christ will be magnified in my body, whether by life or by death.

Col. 4:2-4 ...Continue earnestly in prayer...praying also for us, that God would open to us a door for the word, to speak the mystery of Christ, for which I am also in chains, that I may make it manifest as I ought to speak.

2 Thess 3:1-2 ... Finally brethren, pray for us, that the word of the Lord may have free course and be glorified, just as it is with you, and that we may be delivered from unreasonable and wicked men; for not all have faith.

Rom 15:31 ... That you strive together with me in your prayer to God for me, that I may be delivered from those in Judea who do not believe...

KEY OBSERVATION: If you want to reach a world, ask for prayer for yourself.

1. Paul does in each of the above requests.
2. Not for the lost, but for his own effectiveness.
3. This is strategic. He has the promises. He is the instrument. He knows God can change and empower him.
4. Effective missionary praying begins with praying for the messenger.
5. We may assume that nothing happens in us or through us without this.

I. If you want to win souls, pray for open doors

Col. 4:2-4 Devote yourselves to prayer, being watchful and thankful. And pray for us, too, that God may open a door for our message, so that we may proclaim the mystery of Christ, for which I am in chains. Pray that I may proclaim it clearly, as I should.

When we pray, expect new openness in a friend, neighbour or city

1 Cor. 16:9 I will tarry in Ephesus until Pentecost. For a great and effective door has opened to me, and there are many adversaries.

2 Cor. 2:12-14 When I came to Troas to preach Christ's gospel, and a door was opened to me by the Lord... Now thanks be to God who always leads us in triumph in Christ, and through us diffuses the fragrance of His knowledge in every place.

> **Prayer Practice in groups of three:**
>
> Pray for an open door (or open hearts) in a place or with a person you currently want to lead to faith in Christ.

II. Pray for courage to reach those without Christ

Eph. 6:19-20 Pray also for me, that whenever I open my mouth, words may be given me so that I will fearlessly make known the mystery of the gospel, for which I am an ambassador in chains. Pray that I may declare it fearlessly, as I should.

Phil. 1:19-22 Yes, and I will continue to rejoice, for I know that through your prayers and the help given by the Spirit of Jesus Christ, what has happened to me will turn out for my deliverance. I eagerly expect and hope that I will in no way be ashamed, but will have sufficient courage so that now as always Christ will be exalted in my body, whether by life or by death. For to me, to live is Christ and to die is gain. If I am to go on living in the body, this will mean fruitful labor for me. Yet what shall I choose? I do not know!

Courage comes when we pray, driving out fear from our hearts

Acts 4:24 So when they heard that, they raised their voice to God with one accord and said: "Lord, you are God"... Now Lord, look on their threats and grant to your servants that with all boldness they may speak your word... And when they had prayed, the place where they were assembled together was shaken; and they were all filled with the Holy Spirit and they spoke the Word of God with boldness.

"The devil trembles when he sees God's weakest child on his knees." -Anonymous

> **Prayer Practice in groups of 3:**
>
> 1. Confess your fear and pray for courage in an area or with a person whom you fear.
> 2. Ask to be filled with God's Spirit and with God's Word.

III. Pray for deliverance

Thes. 3:1-2 Finally, brothers, pray for us that the message of the Lord may spread rapidly and be honored, just as it was with you. And pray that we may be delivered from wicked and evil men, for not everyone has faith.

Rom. 15:31 Pray that I may be rescued from the unbelievers in Judea and that my service in Jerusalem may be acceptable to the saints there.

When we pray, God will 'deliver us from evil' and opposition to the gospel

Tim. 4:17-18 But the Lord stood at my side and gave me strength, so that through me the message might be fully proclaimed and all the Gentiles might hear it. And I was delivered from the lion's mouth. The Lord will rescue me from every evil attack and will bring me safely to his heavenly kingdom. To him be glory for ever and ever. Amen.

> **PRAYER PRACTICE in groups of three:**
>
> 1. Pray for each other by name for courage in personal spiritual warfare and for deliverance from evil in ongoing battle.
> 2. Pray for leaders in your church for protection and deliverance.

Triad Prayers: Pray For Open Doors With Your Seeker Friends

"Then Agrippa said to Paul, "Do you think that in such a short time you can persuade me to be a Christian?" Paul replied, "Short time or long—I pray God that not only you but all who are listening to me today may become what I am, except for these chains." Acts 26:28-29

If we recognize that God is the real missionary in evangelism, we see that prayer is the real work. Reaching people with the gospel and introducing them to Jesus must be rooted in continual prayer. The Holy Spirit must go before us in our witness. As we align with God's heart through prayer, he changes our hearts towards others, and we grow in confidence in him to engage their hearts with his living presence.

In your prayer accountability triads, each of you will focus your prayers on three seekers that you are intentionally concentrating your prayer, hospitality, and evangelism efforts on. These are people for whom you feel a burden. You are praying for consistent opportunities to connect with and love in a bold and intentional witness in prayer, deed, and Word.

Pray for ideas and, most importantly, divine appointments, and open doors. Follow through with love and intentionality. Pray for opportunities to let them know you are praying for them, and for open doors to pray *with* them.

As you pray for people, God will give you his heart for them. He will answer the prayers he lays on your heart. As you pray for open doors as Paul did (Col. 4:3), you should find that this is one request that God is eager to answer.

Prayer Friendship Skill
PRAY FOR THE HEARTS OF YOUR SEEKER FRIENDS

Identify three non-Christians in your relational field. Begin committed prayers for them. Ask: How can you pray to know their hearts? Pray for the beauty and brokenness for each person.

SEEKER 1:

BEAUTY:

What does Jesus LOVE about them?

LOVE Beauty

BROKENNESS:

What makes Jesus (and you) SAD to weep for them?

SAD Brokenness

BROKENNESS:

What IDOLS and SINS enslave them?

SINS + IDOLS Brokenness

RESPONSE

How can I respond by *praying the gospel* into their heart?

What *open doors of hospitality* can I serve them in love?

GOSPEL PRAYER Response

OPEN DOORS of HOSPITALITY Response

ENGAGE THE CONVERSATION with God, with believers, with seekers | WWW.PRAYERCURRENT.COM

PRAYER PRACTICE

In groups of three, shar this profile and pray with and for one of each other's friends.

Praise Jesus for his love for them. Thank him for their strengths.

Confess for and cry out for their brokenness. Pray for Christ to stir and meet their deepest need.

Pray for wisdom and compassion in knowing and loving them well.

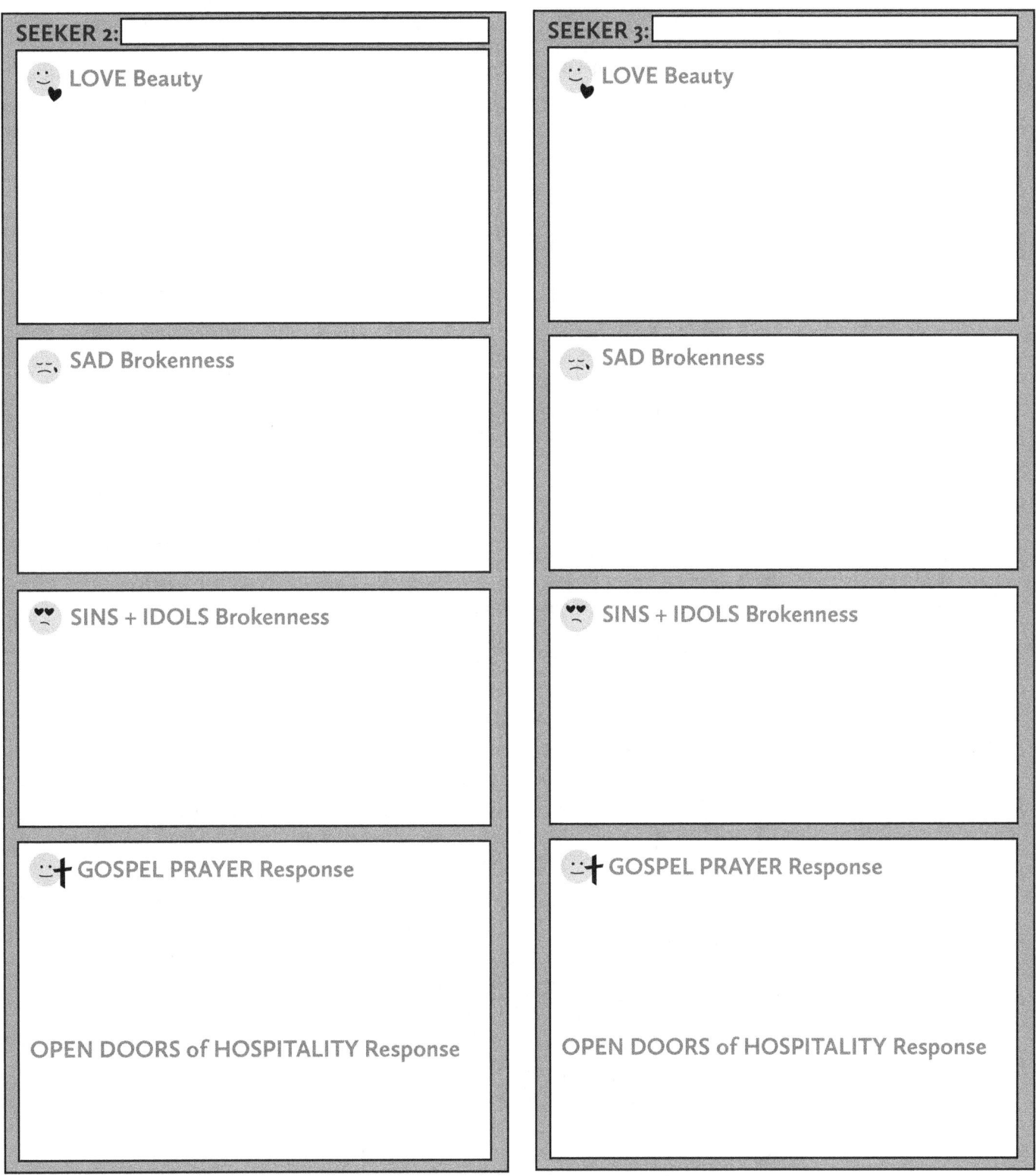

Testimony

THE POWER OF PRAYER ADOPTION AND HOSPITALITY

Testimony from Kevin Rogers, Redeemer Community Church, New Brunswick

During Lent I challenged our small congregation to give something away, in addition to giving something up.

First I asked them to give away prayers for some non-Christian, or unchurched friend. Too often when we share prayer requests what we share are requests for ourselves and our family. These are worthwhile prayers, but we often lack sustained, ongoing prayer for lost friends and neighbours.

We committed to Prayer Adoption – each of us "adopted" 1-3 unchurched friends to pray for every daily.

And two weeks things began to happen. First the young woman that one lady had been praying for her told her that she felt like she had been running away from God, and had abandoned Him. She wanted help as she began a spiritual journey that she had abandoned years ago and now didn't know where to begin.

Then a second woman told me how the family she was praying for, lifelong Roman Catholics although no longer active in the church, asked her "out of the blue" if it was possible for someone who wasn't protestant to attend our church "and just listen."

A third told me how the Muslim co-worker he had been praying for had accepted his invitation for their families to get together, and the conversation naturally flowed into spiritual matters. And then a man I had prayed for four years, stopped me in the hallway of the YMCA to ask about our church and wanted to know what time our Easter Sunday service would be.

Over the past two weeks, I have heard of people taking meals to those that they had "adopted", stopping in to visit new immigrants in their neighbourhood, and of more spiritual conversations taking place between our community and their non-Christian friends than I have ever heard of before. Ever!

The second thing I asked people to give away was an act of kindness. We packed up gift baskets of food treats, Bible and gospel handouts, and an invitation to our church. Each was personalized for a person we focused our "prayer adoption". All this week our people have been delivering these gift baskets in person to the people that they have been praying for. More reports continue to come in of how God has blessed this endeavour.

Readings

YOUR WILL BE DONE ON EARTH

Chapter 4 from *Journey in Prayer*

God's will is rich, deep, and multifaceted. In its most comprehensive sense, God's will is the environment within which all creatures exist. When Jesus asserts that God's will is "done in heaven," he means that God's will is the symphony to which all heaven and its myriad angelic hosts are tuned. This music is so vast and deep and rich that all the songs of heaven are a part of it. God created the world, *"while the morning stars sang together and all the angels shout for joy." (Job 38:7)* Think of the world's great symphonies – The Planets, The Pastoral Symphony, The Four Seasons. Throw in Purcell's Trumpet Voluntary and imagine all rolled into one harmonious, beautiful and joyous song.

We are to do God's will on earth "as in heaven" because God's angels in heaven are in perfect harmony with God's will. Thousands and thousands of angels are in *"joyful assembly"* (*Hebrews 12:22*) because they are tuned to God's will. The cherubim – awesome angelic beings who surround God's throne – are so tuned to God's will that their very movements are in synch with God, *"Wherever the Spirit goes they will go." (Ezekiel 1:20)*

If we are to carry out God's will on earth as in heaven, it is more than a matter of simple obedience. We need to share the angels' inner harmony with the will of God. Our wills need to be tuned to God's will. This is the transformational goal of this command. The apostle Paul points us in this direction:

Do not conform any longer to the pattern of this world, but be transformed by the renewing of your mind. Then you will be able to test and approve what God's will is – his good pleasing and perfect will. (Romans 12:2-3)

Yet the reality is that his will is not done "on earth." From earliest history, there is a dissonance on earth because we have edited God from the songs of our lives. This dissonance manifests itself as exploitation, propaganda, violence, cruelty, and all other forms of injustice. It has spread through all places through all history.

Yet God does not surrender his song to this discord.

He renews the concert of his will – his perfect plan and purpose – to centre stage in history. When Jesus comes to the stable in Bethlehem, on earth we hear heaven's music once again:

Suddenly a great company of the heavenly host appeared with the angel, praising God and saying, "Glory to God in the highest and on earth peace to men on whom his favor rests." (Luke 2:13)

When Jesus surrenders his life on a Roman cross, we imagine a song of lament, funeral eulogy, as the earth itself groans and the skies mourn in darkness. This song is so heart-rending and sorrowful that to hear it is to remember it forever.

When Jesus rises from the dead, we spring from the minor key. We hear the pizzicato of the strings, the dance of the woodwinds and uproarious thunder of the percussion. Our hearts leap and creation dances to the triumphant chorus. This song spreads in overwhelming joy and healing, "as far as the curse is found."

Sing to the LORD a new song;
sing to the LORD, all the earth.

Sing to the LORD, praise his name;
proclaim his salvation day after day.

Let the heavens rejoice, let the earth be glad;
let the sea resound, and all that is in it,

Let the fields be jubilant, and everything in them.
Then all the trees of the forest will sing for joy;

They will sing before the LORD,
for he comes, he comes to judge the earth.
He will judge the world in righteousness and
the peoples in his truth.

  (Psalm 96:1,2,11,13)

When we pray, "Your will be done on earth as it is in heaven," we are asking to once again hear the symphony of God's will. We want to tune our lives to this music and to become a joyous part of its song. We want to obey God, but we want to do it with a song of joy and thanks in our heart.

The scope of this prayer

When we ask that "your will be done on earth as it is in heaven," we pray for at least three things. First, we ask to accept God's will. Second, we pray to approve God's will. Third, we pray to do God's will.

First we pray to accept God's will

God's will is done – always and everywhere. To try to live outside God's will is impossible. His will permeates all existence. In one sense, to oppose God's will is futile. We cannot break God's will – in the sense of preventing him from doing what he decides to do. We can only be broken in the attempt.

An ancient pagan king of Babylon, Nebuchadnezzar, found out about God's unbreakable will the hard way. One day he decides to take credit for his kingdom glory. As he walks the palace walls and surveys Babylon and all its splendors – perhaps looking at the hanging gardens, he boasts:

Is not this the great Babylon I have built as the royal residence, by my mighty power and for the glory of my majesty? (Daniel 4:30)

For this pride, Nebuchadnezzar was stripped of his throne and made to crawl on all fours until his hair looked like eagle's feathers and his claws like bird's claws. When he finally wakes up to his folly, the first thing he proclaims throughout his kingdom is nothing and no one can stop God from doing what he chooses to do:

His dominion is an eternal dominion; his kingdom endures from generation to generation. All the peoples of the earth are regarded as nothing. He does as he pleases with the powers of heaven and the peoples of the earth. No one can hold back his hand or say to him: *"What have you done?" (Daniel 4:33-35)*

Therefore, when we pray, "Your will be done" we affirm that God's rule and reign extends everywhere. We accept the limitation of our freedom when we pray "your will be done." Only God is absolutely free and undetermined.

Our God is in heaven; he does whatever pleases him. (Psalm 115:3)

Everything in heaven and earth is created. God alone is creator. Every creature is dependent on the creation. He stands above the creation in his self-determination and freedom. Our freedom is limited by our nature, our environment, and by God's plan and purposes.

Therefore, when we pray "Your will be done" we worship God and ensure that all of our plans and purposes begin and end with "Deo Volenti" – "God willing."

Second, we ask to approve God's will

When we accept God's will we do not just resign ourselves to it. God's will is not fate. His will is a living expression of his being and reveals his wisdom, justice, and truth. Once we get to know God's will and to accept it, we soon learn to approve it:

Do not conform any longer to the pattern of this world, but be transformed by the renewing of your mind. Then you will be able to test and approve what God's will is – his good, pleasing, and perfect will.
(Romans 12:2-3)

Approving God's will is not always easy. Consider how the biblical character Job interprets God's will. Catastrophe strikes Job from all sides. He loses his property to looters, his animals to fire, and his children to a freak storm. What Job says reveals that he accepts and approves God's will:

At this, Job got up and tore his robe and shaved his head. Then he fell to the ground in worship and said: *"Naked I came from my mother's womb, and naked I will depart. The LORD gave and the LORD has taken away; may the name of the LORD be praised." (Job 1:20-22)* In all this, Job did not sin by charging God with wrongdoing.

This is not resignation. Job does not believe in fate. He knows that God's will is over every event of his life. He knows that God is not capricious or malicious, in spite of how circumstances appear. He believes that God has a higher purpose, even if Job cannot discern it.

Nor does Job believe he is being punished for his sins. He lives by grace and not by karma. When his "friends" insist that he is getting what he deserves, Job maintains that God is not judging him as an offender, but is testing him as his child. To that end he refuses to characterize God as a heartless judge. This is the main theme of Job. He knows that Satan's tempting is God's testing.

This is important. When we pray, "Your will be done," we are asking to understand and approve God's will – especially in the hard times.

The best example of accepting and approving of God's will is Jesus Christ himself. In his final days on earth, Jesus is in the garden of Gethsemane. He knows what agony is in store for him at the cross. He knows that he will be cruelly murdered. He already feels the burden of mankind's sin. In this terrible moment, Jesus does not just wrestle with fate. In prayer, he struggles with, and within, the will of God:

Then he said to them, "My soul is overwhelmed with sorrow to the point of death. Stay here and keep watch with me." Going a little farther, he fell with his face to the ground and prayed, "My Father, if it is possible, may this cup be taken from me. Yet not as I will, but as you will." (Matthew 26:38-39)

Jesus' sorrow is real, and his pain is intense, yet he realizes that his heavenly father permits his suffering for the highest of purposes – the salvation of a universe!

In the same way, the key to our growth in grace is to pray to approve of God's will for our lives:

I cry out to God, who fulfills his purpose for me.
(Psalm 57:2)

In believing prayer, we learn to connect our present troubles to the good and perfect will of God. We refuse to believe that chance rules our lives. We withstand the temptation to imagine that God is capricious or malicious. We know he has a higher purpose and that he is not dealing with us as our sins deserve. Listen to what Peter the apostle says about God's higher purposes:

Dear friends, do not be surprised at the painful trial you are suffering, as though something strange were happening to you. But rejoice that you participate in the sufferings of Christ, so that you may be overjoyed when his glory is revealed. If you are insulted because of the name of Christ, you are blessed, for the Spirit of glory and of God rests on you. So then, those who suffer according to God's will should commit themselves to their faithful Creator and continue to do good. (1 Peter 4:12-19)

As we bring our troubles to Jesus in prayer – asking his will to be done – we approve the will of our Father in heaven. We see our sufferings in the greater reality of his good, acceptable, and perfect will. In prayer we "turn crisis to Christ." Our heart becomes tuned to his heart and we sing the song of grace.

This is good news when it comes to prayer! Once we learn to accept and approve of God's will, we are able to pray with great effect and assurance. When we ask according to God's will, our will is tuned and in harmony with his will. We not only know God's will from the Bible, we have learned to approve his will from our spiritual growth and experience. Jesus calls this harmony with God's will "abiding."

I am the vine; you are the branches...If you abide in me and my words remain in you, ask whatever you wish, and it will be given you. This is to my Father's glory, that you bear much fruit, showing yourselves to be my disciples. (John 15:5,7,8)

Those who abide in Jesus learn to pray according to God's will, and have an inner assurance that their prayers are answered.

Third, we pray to do God's will on earth as in heaven

God's will is perfect. His will is unchangeable but is living and alive as God is. In order to make his will clear, God has given us commands as a rule and guide for life. He requires our obedience to his laws.

Once again, heaven is our example. The chief joy of the angels is to obey God's commands. In fact, we have no biblical examples of angels acting independently of Gods' commands:

The Lord has established his throne in heaven, and his Kingdom rules over all. Praise the Lord, you his angels, you mighty ones who do his bidding and obey his word. Praise the Lord, all his heavenly hosts, you his servants who do his will. (Psalm 103:19-21)

For us to pray and do God's will "as in heaven" we are not to obey God grudgingly, but to rejoice in obeying God.

God's commands are more than rules. Rules are simply legal boundaries. They are impersonal. Consider sporting events. The referee who executes the rules does not have to feel passionate about them. God's commands, in contrast, are not just rules. They express his holy character. They express his identity. God is not a disinterested referee who just makes sure the game is kept "in hand." He is passionate about his laws – for them to be kept – from the heart.

God's will includes a passion for justice. His will includes grief and sorrow for victims of injustice. To do God's will in its fullest sense, is more than mere obedience. True obedience includes sharing his passion for justice and his compassion for victims of injustice. God is internally committed to justice. In fact, justice is an attribute of God. His laws are supremely just. He appoints those who have authority in family, society and church to maintain justice and stop oppression.

Cruelty and injustice happen every day in every city. Women and children are molested. Many are physically abused – in their own homes. Innocent parties are left in ruins after ugly divorce battles. New immigrants are subject to prejudice and given demeaning work. The mentally ill are sent out of crowded hospitals and left to fend for themselves on the streets. From their deepest heart, each victim cries questions of anguish: "Is my suffering God's will? Does God care? Is there justice? Will God rescue me from my oppressor?"

When we ask to do God's will, we commit to listen to these kinds of questions. We ask to know and to share God's passion for justice and his grief at injustice. We pray to hear the cries of the victim and ask to be willing to be the answer. Our prayer for God's will, therefore, is effective only if we share God's love of justice and hatred of oppression, exploitation, and violence.

Deeds are an outcome of prayer

It is not enough to just know God's will, or to pray for God's will to be done, we need grace and courage to obey and carry it out. The rubber has to hit the road. This is the "earth" where Jesus' will is to be done.

When we pray, "Your will be done on earth as it is in heaven," we are committing to doing God's will. Facing the enormous social problems in our cities today, we do not say, "What has this got to do with me? This is the government's job." We cannot say, "This is not my problem. This is part of the wickedness of the world. I am separate from that. I have to protect and preserve my righteousness." Instead we pray, "Your will be done in me and through me." We pray for wisdom and courage to get involved with our city. God gives us wisdom. He will raise up leaders and servants to do his will.

In a Showers for the Shelterless program, we partner with others in our community to serve the homeless and mentally ill. We provide a gourmet coffee, breakfast, and newspaper for our homeless guests. We visit and get to know them. We provide a "valet service" for their shopping carts and dogs. The homeless won't come in if their belongings are unattended.

At a local housing project, we have worked with More Than a Roof to bring the gospel and community development to the tenants who live there. With Genesis Vancouver, a ministry to sexually exploited women and their children, we pray for and seek to serve the sexually exploited – to deliver them not only from pimps and "Johns" but also from a culture that exploits us all. We partner and pray for Genesis Vancouver to provide safe houses and day programs for the sexually exploited and their children.

There is a connection between our praying for justice and justice coming to pass. Speaking to Israel while exiled in Babylon, Jeremiah reminds his people to seek justice for their city.

Seek the peace and prosperity of the city to which I carried you in exile. Pray to the Lord for it, because if it prospers, you too will prosper...For I know the plans I have for you, declares the Lord, plans to prosper you and not to harm you, plans to give you hope and a future. Then you will call upon me and I will listen to you. (Jeremiah 29:7,11,12)

Notice how prayer for the city is commanded. Notice how God promises he will answer with urban peace and prosperity.

Another striking passage is found in Isaiah 58. As in Jeremiah, there is a connection between our prayers for urban renewal and God's promise to hear this prayer. However, something crucial is added. God's answer to our prayer is that he sends us into the city to be his agents of transformation. He will rebuild the city. He will do it through those who pray. We become the answer to our own prayer!

Is this not the kind of fasting that I have chosen: to loose the chains of injustice and untie the cords of the yoke, to set the oppressed free and break every yoke? Is it not to share your food with the hungry and to provide the poor wanderer with shelter ...Then your light will break forth like the dawn and your healing will quickly appear; then your righteousness will go before you and the glory of the Lord will be your rear guard. Then you will call and the Lord will answer; you will cry for help and he will say Here am I...Your people will rebuild the ancient ruins and will raise up the age old foundations; you will be called Repairer of Broken Walls, Restorer of Streets with Dwellings. (Isaiah 58)

The implication is clear. As God's people we are to pray for his will to be done on earth. We are to become deeply engaged with the needs of our city. God will answer our prayer as we do so. He will rescue the needy and establish safe neighborhoods. The way God renews the city is by sending his people to carry out this mandate. This is how his will is done on earth as it is in heaven.

Let it sink in. Let it take your breath away. As we seek God's will in prayer, and then carry it out, we will embody the transformation the oppressed cry out for! We will see substantial healing and restoration at the heart of our city. What a marvelous encouragement to prayer.

 *Bring it Home*

Pray It Forward:

    Personal prayer at home:

- Review your Oikos circles. Commit these people to God in prayer.
- Ask God who he would have you focus your prayers on.
- Complete your spiritual analysis for friends and pray for open hearts: How can I pray to know their hearts? Pray for open doors into their hearts and lives, spiritually and practically.
- Pray for divine appointments – with your seeker friends, and new people in the wider Oikos circle.

Share It Outward

    Prayer and practice steps with others:

1. Meet with your triad (from this class, in person or by phone or online) to pray for seeker friends.
2. Reach out to meet one of your 3 seeker friends (for a get together, phone conversation, or act of kindness, etc.)
    - Ask questions to know them beyond the surface. Practice being present, listening for how they might need prayer. Listen to their heart.

Readings:

- Read ahead and prepare Week 6.

WEEK SIX

Team Up with Mission Prayer Partners

The Power Of United And Persevering Prayer

According to Paul, when it comes to sharing your faith, you need more than the right words: *"The Kingdom of God does not consist of talk but of power."* (1 Corinthians 4:14). God's power is at the heart of effective witness to Christ. Every believer has the indwelling power of God. The apostle prays for the church at Ephesus to discover and experience Christ's power.

> *I pray that you may know...what is the immeasurable greatness of his power toward us who believe, according to the working of his great might 20 that he worked in Christ when he raised him from the dead... 20 Now to him who is able to do far more abundantly than all that we ask or think, according to the power at work within us, 21 to him be glory in the church and in Christ. (Ephesians 1:19,20, 3:20,21)*

We all have God's power at work within us. Yet, the experience of God's power is not automatic! This power is unlocked by prayer. It is especially when we join together in earnest and united prayer that we experience answers to prayer and the Holy Spirit's power to speak the gospel.

Jesus promises that our united prayers will be met with answers. As we pray together, we can win over those who stray:

> *19 Again I say to you, if two of you agree on earth about anything they ask, it will be done for them by my Father in heaven. 20 For where two or three are gathered in my name, there am I among them." (Matthew 18:19,20)*

Before he ascends to the right hand of God, Jesus promises power to his followers,*"Wait, you shall receive power when the Holy Spirit comes upon you and you will be my witnesses."* (Acts 1:4,8). These followers wait in prayer for ten days, *"constantly joined together in prayer."* At the end of this time, the place is shaken by an earthquake; the Holy Spirit comes upon and fills each one (Acts 2:1-4). A community of love, prayer, and power results (Acts 2:42-47). The disciples *"preach the word of God with boldness."* Three thousand come to Christ in one day.

This is repeated several times in the book of Acts. Whenever God's people join in earnest and united kingdom prayer, God pours out his power.

After intense persecution of the church we read:

> *They lifted their voices together to God... and when they had prayed, the place in which they were gathered together was shaken, and they were all filled with the Holy Spirit and continued to speak the word of God with boldness. (Acts 4:31-37).*

The community of love and joy grows to five thousand men, plus women and children.

Time and again in the early church, prayer ignites mission.

In Acts 12:5-10, we read of a church praying through the night. Not only was Peter miraculously delivered from prison and a death sentence, the city gates open wide for renewed gospel proclamation! the chains felll off...they passed the first and second guard...

> *So Peter was kept in prison, but earnest prayer for him was made to God by the church.... on that very night, Peter was sleeping between two soldiers, bound with two chains, and sentries before the door were guarding the prison. 7 And behold, an angel of the Lord stood next to him, and a light shone in the cell. He struck Peter on the side and woke him, saying, "Get up quickly." And the chains fell off his hands.... When they had passed the first and the second guard, they came to the iron gate leading into the city. It opened for them of its own accord. vs 5-10*

We cannot be effective in sharing the gospel of Christ without praying together for power. We dare not try.

One last example illustrates that God gives power and direction to those who unite in earnest prayer. When the leaders of the Antioch church unite in prayer, they discover the greater plan and purpose of God:

> *While they were worshiping the Lord and fasting, the Holy Spirit said, "Set apart for me Barnabas and Saul for the work to which I have called them."...So, being sent out by the Holy Spirit, they went down to Seleucia. (Acts 13:1-4)*

When we unite in earnest united prayer, the Holy Spirit assumes his rightful role as the Lord of His mission. This certainty gives power and assurance to the church leaders of that day. The Spirit's power and direction is promised to his praying church today.

Scripture Study

1. In prayer we discover and experience the power of God

I pray that you may know...what is the immeasurable greatness of his power toward us who believe, according to the working of his great might 20 that he worked in Christ when he raised him from the dead... 20 Now to him who is able to do far more abundantly than all that we ask or think, according to the power at work within us, 21 to him be glory in the church and in Christ.
(Ephesians 1:19,20, 3:20,21)

On your own:

Describe what the power of God means to you.

What does it look like when God's power is active in your life?

PRAYER PRACTICE: Pray for a fresh discovery and enjoyment of the power of God in your life.

2. Jesus makes a special promise to us when we gather in prayer

Again I say to you, if two of you agree on earth about anything they ask, it will be done for them by my Father in heaven. For where two or three are gathered in my name, there am I among them."
(Matthew 18:19,20)

Discuss in groups of three:

What are some of the challenges we face when it comes to joining in 'earnest united prayer'?

Suggest practical solutions.

3. We cannot be effective in sharing the gospel of Christ without praying together for power. We dare not try.

They lifted their voices together to God... and when they had prayed, the place in which they were gathered together was shaken, and they were all filled with the Holy Spirit and continued to speak the word of God with boldness. (Acts 4:31-37).

So Peter was kept in prison, but earnest prayer for him was made to God by the church....When they came to the iron gate leading into the city. It opened for them of its own accord. (Acts 12:5,10)

Discuss in groups of three:

How have you experienced the influence of prayer (or lack of prayer) on your effectiveness in sharing your faith?

Share any examples of how you have seen prayer affect the church's effective corporate witness of Christ.

What happens when we try to go ahead with the mission without uniting in prayer?

PRAYER PRACTICE:

Pray together: Thank God for strengths in witness/ confess your weaknesses.
Ask Jesus to bring his people together to pray.

EVALUATE YOUR PERSONAL AND CHURCH PRAYER PROGRESS

1=weak, 5=strong

- 1 2 3 4 5   I experience a growing relationship with Christ as I pray
- 1 2 3 4 5   When facing crisis and discouragement, I pray through the challenges to find Christ (eg. relational breakdown, depression, loneliness, financial panic, dryness, etc.)
- 1 2 3 4 5   I pray beyond my own needs (for non-Christians, for my city, and the world)
- 1 2 3 4 5   I meet with others to pray on a regular basis (1 on 1, small group, prayer meetings, etc.)
- 1 2 3 4 5   I engage in regular extended times/days of prayer.
- 1 2 3 4 5   Our prayer times (family, church, ministry, etc.) are energized by a balance of kingdom priorities (worship, outreach, confession, pastoral care, etc.)
- 1 2 3 4 5   We respond to crisis with united prayer (eg. marital strife, gossip, financial crisis, etc.)
- 1 2 3 4 5   Our meetings are as much about waiting in prayer, as they are about planning
- 1 2 3 4 5   We train our ministry leaders (disciples, children, followers) in kingdom prayer
- 1 2 3 4 5   We engage in regular extended times/days of corporate prayer
- 1 2 3 4 5   We pray beyond our own urgencies, for non-Christians to come to Christ, for our community and the world
- 1 2 3 4 5   Growth in our ministries, outreaches, and conversions are traced to and empowered by prayer.

Summarize strengths and encouragements to praise God for.

Summarize weaknesses to confess, surrender and trust God to address.

What are your specific challenges to growing in prayer? Brainstorm practical ideas to address them, including more importantly, by prayer.

PRAYER PRACTICE:
- Praise God for encouragements and evidences seen of growth in corporate prayer.
- Confess and surrender weaknesses.
- Ask the Spirit to pour out a spirit of grace and supplication.

ENGAGE THE CONVERSATION with God, with believers, with seekers | WWW.PRAYERCURRENT.COM

PRAYING THE LORD'S PRAYER

Implications for uniting in prayer:

> *Pray then like this:*
> *"Our Father in heaven, hallowed be your name.*
> *Your kingdom come,*
> *your will be done, on earth as it is in heaven.*
> *Give us this day our daily bread,*
> *and forgive us our debts, as we also have forgiven our debtors.*
> *And lead us not into temptation, but deliver us from evil.*

On your own, reflect:

The pronouns in Jesus prayer are plural. What are the implications for your prayer life?

Compare Jesus' prayer with your prayers. Note similarities and differences.

PRAYER PRACTICE: Commit your insights to prayer.

Discuss in groups of 3:

The pronouns in Jesus prayer are plural. What are the implications for our corporate prayer life?

Compare Jesus' prayer with church prayer times. Note similarities and differences.

PRAYER PRACTICE

Pray for Christ to bless his people in praying his prayer. Take turns, praying the prayer line, by line, with one person praying through one line, and passing it to the next.

Readings

GIVE US THIS DAY OUR DAILY BREAD

Chapter 5 from *Journey in Prayer*

"Give us this day our daily bread" are simple words that summarize all our prayers for earthly concerns. "Bread" is more than food. It also refers to the Word of God. Jesus said, "Man does not live by bread alone but by every word that proceeds from the mouth of God." (Matthew 4:4) Bread refers to the enjoyment of the gospel and faith in God.

It is also a metaphor for all of life's necessities. When we ask for daily bread we ask for good government and good health. We also ask for good health, so that we can enjoy our food. Robbie Burns penned a prayer:

Some ha' meat that canna' eat.
Some na' ha' meat that want it.
We ha' meat, and we ca' eat
Sa the Lord be thanked.

When we pray for daily bread, our request has a specific meaning as well as a comprehensive application. We are asking for all of life's necessities as well as the peace and health to enjoy them.

Asking for daily bread slowly changes our entire outlook on life

As we pray this amazing prayer we not only receive what we ask for – bread – we also discover that Jesus is transforming us. First, he is teaching us trust and thankfulness. Second, he is building generosity and kindness. Third, Jesus is developing our contentment and simplicity of life. We become what we pray.

1. As we pray, we learn trust and thankfulness

As we humbly ask, "Give us this day our daily bread," we acknowledge that all good things come from God. When we credit our own labor and industry for the prosperity we enjoy, we are denying that life is a gift.

In Canada, a wealthy person puts in a long day to make a good living. In Calcutta, a rickshaw driver works day and night to make a few rupees. If a person is poor, it often has nothing to do with how industrious he is. He or she may not have the opportunity to make a good living.

When we pray for bread, "we lift up empty hands." We depend on God to fill all our needs from his own bounty and kindness. Asking for daily bread involves turning from self-reliance and asking for a heart that relies on God.

Trust in God's provision is enriched with thankfulness of heart

The habit of asking implies a response of thanksgiving. There is no greater proof of Jesus' work in our hearts than genuine thankfulness. Thanksgiving is an antidote to greed and to envy. When we give thanks we take our eyes off what we do not have.

Just as the world looks smaller from the window of a plane at 35,000 feet, in thankful prayer we rise above daily problems and see the abundance of God. It is amazing how discontent with the bills, mortgage, and expenses of life disappears when we give thanks for the abundance on our table each day.

Achieving thankfulness is at the heart of Jesus' plan for his people. When the Israelites returned from the Babylonian captivity and rebuilt the city walls, their leaders "assigned two large choirs to give thanks." (Nehemiah 12:31)

To the believers at Philippi Paul explains how thankfulness cures worry:

Do not be anxious about anything, but in everything, by prayer and petition, with thanksgiving, present your requests to God. And the peace of God, which transcends all understanding, will guard your hearts and your minds in Christ Jesus. (Philippians 4:6,7)

As we pray, we move from anxiety and restlessness about possessions to a spirit of "joyfully giving thanks." When we start our day, or begin a meal with simple thankfulness, we are cultivating an attitude of contentment and inner joy.

2. As we pray, we learn kindness and generosity

We do not ask, "Give me this day my daily bread." We pray, "give us this day our daily bread." This is a prayer for others as much as it is a prayer for ourselves. We also pray for our friends, neighbors, family – indeed, our country and whole world – to have daily bread.

We love our neighbor in prayer. We are also to love our neighbor in deeds:

If anyone has material possessions and sees his brother in need but has no pity on him, how can the love of God be in him? No one can say they love God, whom they cannot see, if they do not love their brother whom they do see. (1John 4:20)

Jesus' parable of the Good Samaritan teaches us never to discriminate when it comes to compassion and kindness. The wounded and naked person on the roadside is Jewish. While Jewish religious types walk by the other side of the road, the Samaritan – whose people were sworn enemies of the Jews – bandages and feeds his enemy. This foreigner's love for God is evidenced in his compassion. (Luke 10)

When we pray this prayer we ask for a generous spirit

When we ask for daily bread, we ask for the ability and willingness to give an increasing portion of what we have to others in need. Jesus says, "Freely you have received. Freely give." No matter how much we make or own, we ask to be content with a modest portion. We pray for courage and integrity to give sacrificially to Christ's mission and to those in need.

Christian giving is sacrificial because it is modeled on the sacrifice of Jesus:

For you know the grace of our Lord Jesus Christ, that though he was rich, yet for your sakes he became poor, so that you through his poverty might become rich. (2 Corinthians 8:9)

Jesus says, "Love your neighbor as yourself." This means we should love and care for ourselves as well as for our neighbor. Life is meant to be lived in balance. Our life is a "mini Trinity" of relationships – God, others and self. A balanced person divides and balances his or her time, energy and resources on God first, others second, and self third.

However, anything near this balance is rare. On average, each of us spends more than 95 per cent of life's income on ourselves. No matter how we slice it, this is not a life of balance. There is too little left for God and others.

This lack of balance leads to ill health and a poor state of mind. We can trace a good deal of spiritual unhappiness and discontent to a preoccupation with self. As we follow Jesus in day-by-day prayer for bread, God will lead us to a life of kindness and generosity – to a life of balance.

3. As we pray we learn contentment and simplicity

When we ask God for "this day's" bread, we are called to seek God's provision one day at a time. We leave tomorrow to him.

This is the lesson of the manna.

The children of Israel are led through a wilderness for forty years. God provides them daily bread – called manna. It contains everything they need in the way of nourishment. However, it only lasts that day. It rots overnight.

God provides his children a lesson of daily trust in this. He teaches the Israelites to look to him one day at a time to give them all they need. When we ask "this day" for bread, we ask for a portion of life's blessings that is enough for this day. We do not ask for too little – so that we unable pay our bills, provide for our dependents, and help those in need. Yet, we ask for bread, not a life of luxury and indulgence.

When we ask for daily bread, we leave it in God's hands to decide how much or how little is right for us. He can take us through times of want and scarcity. We may have savings accounts, insurance, and retirement plans, but if we are not careful these "storehouses" become a substitute for daily reliance upon God!

Jesus tells us a simple and powerful parable about this "storehouse" problem:

"The ground of a certain rich man produced a good crop. He thought to himself, 'What shall I do? I have no place to store my crops.' "Then he said, 'This is what I'll do. I will tear down my barns and build bigger ones, and there I will store all my grain and my goods. And I'll say to myself, "You have plenty of good things laid up for many years. Take life easy; eat, drink and be merry." "But God said to him, 'You fool! This very night your life will be demanded from you. Then who

will get what you have prepared for yourself?' "This is how it will be with anyone who stores up things for himself but is not rich toward God." (Luke 12:16-21)

God knows what each of his children can handle. God knows what we need.

He knows how much we need. He has a perfect plan for us. Poverty or riches is not the issue – contentment is. Just look, he says, at the world he has created:

Therefore I tell you, do not worry about your life, what you will eat or drink; or about your body, what you will wear.... Look at the birds of the air; they do not sow or reap or store away in barns, and yet your heavenly Father feeds them. Are you not much more valuable than they? Who of you by worrying can add a single hour to his life? And why do you worry about clothes? See how the lilies of the field grow. They do not labor or spin. Yet I tell you that not even Solomon in all his splendor was dressed like one of these. But seek first his kingdom and his righteousness, and all these things will be given to you as well. Therefore do not worry about tomorrow, for tomorrow will worry about itself. Each day has enough trouble of its own. (Matthew 6:25-29,33-34)

Each time I pray this prayer for daily bread, I take time to thank God for the various kinds of "daily bread" I enjoy. I ask God to help me to trust him one day at a time. I ask him to forgive and still my restless need to store up for tomorrow.

Asking for "bread" encourages a life of simplicity

Bread is wonderful. Walk into any bakery early in the morning and you know what I mean. The aroma stirs every hungry cell. Yet bread is the simplest of foods.

In this petition we ask to live with increasing simplicity. Simplicity is difficult for us. When we sell a house at a good profit, inherit some money, or receive a raise or bonus, without thinking, we immediately plan how to spend or save it. We make our lives more cluttered than before! In our aptly named "consumer culture," this habit of increased acquisition seems obvious and right. In contrast, Jesus' call to simplicity seems quaint or absurd.

However, following Jesus and praying this prayer has radical consequences. Simplicity becomes a beautiful thing. Luxury and self-indulgence become ugly.

Bring it Home

Pray It Forward

Personal prayer at home:

- Pray about your own prayer life with others.
- Pray over your Oikos map.
- Pray the Lord's Prayer for each of your seeker friends.

Share it Outward

Prayer and practice steps with others:

1. Pray with your triad. Meet with two others (from this class, in person or by phone or online) to pray for your Oikos and your seeker friends.

2. Reach out to meet one of your 3 seeker friends (for a get together, phone conversation, or act of kindness, etc.)
   - Continue in friendly 'listening' conversation- seek opportunities to share your current experience learning about prayer with friends.
   - Tell them you have been praying for them...Ask questions to know them beyond the surface. Practice being present, listening for how they might need prayer. Listen to their heart. Ask if they have specific requests.

3. Meet with someone who is marginalized/ lonely/international/ refugee

- Show them kind hospitality (and resolve to continue the relationship)
- If you have opportunity, ask/listen/talk about what you are learning about prayer about Jesus.

Readings:

- Read ahead and prepare Week 7.

WEEK SEVEN

Bring God into the Conversation with a Seeker Friend

God conversations are good for the soul. Time after time, I've found it is interesting and creative to talk about God. We've all had interesting and creative conversations about God. It's a great way to deepen relationships. Most importantly, God conversations are the chief way many people get to get to know God.

If God is in a conversation, It isn't a technique. Technique bypasses people. If it becomes a technique you can be sure God isn't in the conversation.

If you would know how to bring God into the conversation these suggestions might help you.

1. LOVE PEOPLE.

There is no one so disagreeable that you can't value him or her. Each person is made in God's image. (Genesis 1:24-26)

'We must not brood on the wickedness of man, but realize he is God's image bearer. If we cover and obliterate man's faults and consider the beauty and dignity of God's image in him, then we shall be induced to love and embrace him.' (From The Golden Booklet of the Christian Life)

Jesus loves people. When he looks at the 'maddening crowd' he does not despise their need.

He looks past their obvious faults.

"He had compassion on them because they were harassed and helpless, like sheep without a shepherd." (Matthew 9:35 ff.)

2. EXPECT TO MAKE A FRIEND.

Friendship is built one great conversation on another.

Some say, "Don't discuss religion or politics if you want to make friends.' I would say the opposite is true. In order to get to know anyone well you need to know what matters to them most – their core beliefs and convictions. Friendship involves openness. What someone believes or does not believe about God is at the heart of who they are. Real friends talk about their beliefs because what they believe matters to them and matters to the friendship.

3. PUT THE PERSON FIRST, NOT THEIR ARGUMENT.

It's people that are interesting, creative, and precious. Their point of view comes second. Get to know someone – in good time you will get to know what they value and believe. You are not winning an argument; you are helping another person on their journey. You are awakening them to their own uniqueness. You might waken them to God.

4. DISCERN WHERE GOD IS SPEAKING.

If someone is seeking ultimate truth, God has put this in his or her heart. "God has put eternity into man's heart," wrote Solomon in Ecclesiastes. If someone is searching, you can be sure God is inviting them to the quest.

5. TELL YOUR STORY; ASK FOR THEIRS.

You telling your story offends no one. Often they are happy to share theirs. Your story is an invitation and a kind way to encourage them to think and respond.

6. EXPECT REVELATIONS AND ENLIGHTENMENT WHILE YOU CONVERSE.

'Revelation' is the English translation of the word 'apocalupto' or apocalypse. It means to pull back the veil and reveal what is hidden. A good conversation opens the door to new vistas of truth, wisdom and knowledge – especially about God.

'Enlightenment' is translated from the Greek <Epiphano>. It means to be surrounded by light. We talk about how 'the light goes on' when a great idea is shared. God conversations often bring enlightenment – the lights go on. You can see it in each other's eyes.

7. BE OPEN ABOUT YOUR BELIEFS AND CONVICTIONS.

A good conversation about God begins by respecting the other person's foundational beliefs. Respect and listening constitutes 'fair play' in any great conversation.

Your convictions of truth are not always evident to the person you converse with. In my case, as a Christian, the axioms of my thoughts come from a theistic worldview.

"Hey that's not fair!" some might argue, "you're using religion." I would say it's only unfair if you deny or hide your beliefs. None of us starts from 'the simple truth.' We all have underlying assumptions and convictions, even if we are no more aware of these than a fish is of the water he swims in.

8. BE INFORMED. GET TO KNOW WHAT OTHERS BELIEVE.

A good conversationalist is a bit of a philosopher. Philosophy means to love knowledge. A philosopher is curious and eager to learn. The alternative is ignorance. Some of the things I have read to deepen my conversations include:

- Thích Nhat Hanh, *The Heart of Buddha's Teaching*
- *Bhagavad Gita*
- *The Koran*
- Writings of Atheists like Voltaire, Nietzsche, Richard Dawkins
- New Age thinkers like Dan Brown
- Scientists like Brian Green
- Defenders of the Christian faith: Blaise Pascal, GK Chesterton, Dorothy Sayers, CS Lewis, Timothy Keller
- Lots of philosophy, several courses at university
- Literature, both classic and contemporary are a great way to discern 'the spirit of the age'
- The Bible. Objectively it is hands down the most formative book of western civilization, and increasingly the rest of the world.

I keep up with science for lay people by reading Scientific American, Discovery and other educational magazines. Brian Green is a great teacher to keep up to date.

As I read, I learn things that delight me. I want to be a lover of learning. As I keep reading I learn more about my own beliefs and am able to converse intelligently about other views.

9. LEARN TO ASK GOOD QUESTIONS.

A good question has a way of awakening us to the quest. For example, Plato shaped all of his writings in the form of dialogues. These dialogues are filled with probing questions. His aim is to lead his hearers to a purer idea of what is true and what is good.

Jesus takes a similar approach. For example, when he meets a Samaritan woman at the well he takes her from surface matters into a deeper conversation. You can find this dialogue in John 4.

Jesus catches her attention by asking her to draw water from the well for him. This question jars her. Why does he ask her to give him water? He wants to awaken her thirst for deeper truths.

"Everyone who drinks of this water will be thirsty again, but whoever drinks of the water that I will give him will never be thirsty again." (John 4:13-14)

Jesus takes her deeper with another question. He asks to meet her husband. She says, "I have no husband."

Jesus said to her, *"You are right in saying, 'I have no husband'; for you have had five husbands, and the one you now have is not your husband. What you have said is true." (John 4:17-18)*

Jesus goes down the well of her life history to help her search her heart. The woman is awakened to the reality underlying the conversation. She simply has to know who he is:

The woman said to him, "I know that Messiah is coming (he who is called Christ). When he comes, he will tell us all things." Jesus said to her, "I who speak to you am he." (John 4:25-26)

The woman at the well has her thirst satisfied.

10. PRAY FOR APPOINTMENTS.

Someone has said, "When I pray, coincidences happen." I find when I pray for the opportunity to bring God into the conversation, I often find my self in the middle of one. This is no accident. It's an appointment. I get to be God's messenger in Him speaking to someone. What a privilege.

God desires all men to come to a knowledge of the truth. (1 Timothy 2:1)

On your own: Choose 2 ideas you find helpful/ you resonate with.

With a friend in mind, write down one or two approaches you will take, as doors open, to bring God in the conversation.

PRAYER PRACTICE:
In groups of 3, share your idea with each other and pray for God to open doors to these God conversations.

Scripture Study

PAUL'S CREATIVE EVANGELISM:
3 Ways to Bring Christ into the Conversation

In the large group, read Acts 16:11-34.

Now in groups of three, each group discuss one of the following passages each. Read and discuss questions. Appoint someone to share key insights with the larger group.

GROUP 1:

To a person familiar with the message (verses 11-15)

¹¹ So, setting sail from Troas, we made a direct voyage to Samothrace, and the following day to Neapolis, ¹² and from there to Philippi, which is a leading city of the [district of Macedonia and a Roman colony. We remained in this city some days. ¹³ And on the Sabbath day we went outside the gate to the riverside, where we supposed there was a place of prayer, and we sat down and spoke to the women who had come together. ¹⁴ One who heard us was a woman named Lydia, from the city of Thyatira, a seller of purple goods, who was a worshiper of God. The Lord opened her heart to pay attention to what was said by Paul. ¹⁵ And after she was baptized, and her house-hold as well, she urged us, saying, "If you have judged me to be faithful to the Lord, come to my house and stay." And she prevailed upon us.

Discuss: How does Paul scout out an opportunity?

How does he adapt to the context?

---

page 79

GROUP 2:

To a victim of men and of Satan (verses 16-18)

16 As we were going to the place of prayer, we were met by a slave girl who had a spirit of divination and brought her owners much gain by fortune-telling. 17 She followed Paul and us, crying out, "These men are servants] of the Most High God, who proclaim to you the way of salvation." 18 And this she kept doing for many days. Paul, having become greatly annoyed, turned and said to the spirit, "I command you in the name of Jesus Christ to come out of her." And it came out that very hour.

Discuss: How does Paul adapt to the context?

How does God precipitate a missionary appointment?

Where does this little girl fit into the drama?

GROUP 3

To an ordinary someone 'not looking for trouble' God does something extraordinary. Paul land Silas are thrown in prison for preaching and for delivering a servant girl from an evil spirit.

25 About midnight Paul and Silas were praying and singing hymns to God, and the prisoners were listening to them, 26 and suddenly there was a great earthquake, so that the foundations of the prison were shaken. And immediately all the doors were opened, and everyone's bonds were unfastened. 27 When the jailer woke and saw that the prison doors were open, he drew his sword and was about to kill himself, supposing that the prisoners had escaped. 28 But Paul cried with a loud voice, "Do not harm yourself, for we are all here." 29 And the jailer[f] called for lights and rushed in, and trembling with fear he fell down before Paul and Silas. 30 Then he brought them out and said, "Sirs, what must I do to be saved?" 31 And they said, "Believe in the Lord Jesus, and you will be saved, you and your household." 32 And they spoke the word of the Lord to him and to all who were in his house. 33 And he took them the same hour of the night and washed their wounds; and he was baptized at once, he and all his family. 34 Then he brought them up into his house and set food before them. And he rejoiced along with his entire household that he had believed in God.

Discuss, what were Paul and Silas praying for? How does God turn the tables.

How does prayer connect to gospel advance in this passage?

In the large group, debrief the highlights of your smaller group discussions.

How should we then pray?

PRAYER PRACTICE:

Pray in groups of 2,3... appy your insights from these passages to your prayers add names of people you know, care for, to pray for....

PRAYING FOR APPOINTMENTS

Col. 4:2-4 Devote yourselves to prayer, being watchful and thankful. And pray for us, too, that God may open a door for our message, so that we may proclaim the mystery of Christ, for which I am in chains. Pray that I may proclaim it clearly, as I should.

1 Cor. 16:9 I will tarry in Ephesus until Pentecost. For a great and effective door has opened to me, and there are many adversaries.

Discuss in groups of three:

What is the importance of praying for appointments?

What does an open door look like? Have you experienced an open door become closed? Or a closed door become open?

Who does God want you to focus your prayers/witness towards? What would an open door or divine appointment look like practically speaking?

PRAYER PRACTICE: Pray for appointments!

A Testimony Of The Importance Of Praying For 'Appointments' To Share The Good News:

One church planter reports asking God for 100 appointments to share his faith in his city in a six week period. The reason for this unusual request was that it was an international festival time and everyone was trading pins. He purchased 120 lapel pins that represented the gospel in a simple five points. By the end of six weeks this evangelist reports having given the pin to some 106 people, each time sharing at least the outline of the gospel. About 30 times the conversation was extended. One time he had a one-hour discussion with two Harley Davidson dealers who wanted to know more about Christianity (because a friend was always trying to share with one of them). Out of 100 'appointments', not one person gave a hostile or even negative response In fact, more than half expressed appreciation. A number entered into deeper discussions. Two Ethiopian Jews enjoyed a long discussion and attended a Bible study that evening.

Readings

FORGIVE US OUR DEBT AS WE FORGIVE OUR DEBTORS

Chapter 6 from *Journey in Prayer*

It is curious that Jesus leaves this urgent necessity towards the end of his prayer. Why did he not start with forgiveness?

In his prayer, Jesus puts God first. He teaches us to do the same. Jesus also wants us to know how to approach God, so we know what to ask forgiveness for. "Our Father" sets the relational context which permits a humble, courageous approach to God – faults and all. If we do not come to God as father, we will tend to approach him as a forbidding judge.

What Needs To Be Forgiven

We need to be forgiven for our sins. But what is sin? There is no easy answer to this question. Seneca said, "Sin is complex and admits infinite variations."

Sin concerns wrong behavior. You know the list – idolatry, murder, promiscuity, stealing, and lying. Yet we know sin goes deeper. It includes our thoughts and motives: hatred, envy, greed, malice, pride, and self-righteousness. Jesus said, "Whoever nurses anger against a brother has committed murder." (Matthew 5:22)

Sin is more than isolated actions or thoughts. All sin is deeply personal and relational. When we sin we offend God, others, and self. Think about it. If we choose another god to worship besides God Almighty, we "cheat" on him. Similarly, when we steal from someone, we undermine our bond with them.

Sin is serious. It wounds people and breaks relationships. The only way to restore these relationships is for Jesus to be wounded and broken for us.

The High Price For Our Forgiveness

After viewing Mel Gibson's The Passion of the Christ, many wondered why Jesus had to suffer so brutally. Hours of whipping, a wreath of thorns, spitting and mocking, hands being nailed to rough sawn wood, all drawn out in painful, graphic detail.

Is this overkill?

The answer is "No!" Forgiveness is free but it is not cheap. The highest price possible is paid that we might receive forgiveness as a free gift. The brutality of the cross is a measure of the horror of human sin. Put all hatred, malice, envy, lust, deceit, betrayal – and all the wars, rapes, genocides, abuse and oppression in humankind's sad history and you will understand the infinite price required and paid to remove our sin and provide forgiveness forever.

Yet, Jesus' death is not a tragedy. His suffering conquers sin and defeats death at the cross. It achieves reconciliation for you when you come to God for forgiveness of any crime, cruelty, or injustice. All you have to do is humbly ask.

When you confess your sins you are completely washed clean of them. An old saying captures this truth:

That Jesus died on the cross is history.
That Jesus died for sin is theology.
That Jesus died for my sin is Christianity.

As you read this, remember why Jesus died. Ask him to apply his sacrifice to you and to forgive your sins. Become the renewed person he died for you to be.

The Challenge Of Receiving Forgiveness

The prick of our conscience often makes us aware of the seriousness of sin. But we need great assurances from God in order to find the humility and courage to confess our sins. We need the promises of God:

Though your sins are like scarlet, they shall be as white as snow; though they are red as crimson, they shall be like wool. (Isaiah 1:18)

If we confess our sins, he is faithful and just and will forgive us our sins and purify us from all unrighteousness. (1 John 1:9)

It takes grace to confess, and grace to receive forgiveness. We struggle with residual guilt, rehearsing our faults again and again. What can we do about our reluctance to receive forgiveness? We must remember these great promises in Scripture. And we must remind ourselves that God forgets our sin once he forgives it.

Forgiveness is as complete and finished as the perfect sacrifice of Jesus. This verse tells how Jesus is the only one who can remove the guilt and the power of sin:

If anybody does sin, we have one who speaks to the Father in our defense—Jesus Christ, the Righteous One. He is the atoning sacrifice for our sins and not only for ours but also for the sins of the whole world. (1 John 2:1-2)

The principle is this – don't dwell on your sin and guilt, but look steadily at Jesus. His sacrifice has infinite value to cancel your debt. Your sins are forever nailed to the cross.

The Challenge And Joy Of Learning To Forgive Others

When we ask for forgiveness it is "as we forgive our debtors." Receiving forgiveness is only half the picture. Jesus teaches that we are to extend forgiveness to others, as well, without exception:

For if you forgive men when they sin against you, your heavenly Father will also forgive you but if you do not forgive men their sins, your Father will not forgive your sins. (Matthew 6:14)

Jesus tells us to forgive without excuse for how often or how deep the offense:

When Peter came to Jesus and asked, "Lord, how many times shall I forgive my brother when he sins against me? Up to seven times?" Jesus answered, "I tell you, not seven times, but seventy-seven times." (Matthew 18:21)

Overlooking a fault is possible in the "misdemeanors" of life. A rough word, minor neglect, or criticism – such wounds often heal in their own time.

What are we to do, however, with the "felonies" of life? Consider victims of adultery and wrongful divorce. Or those who are defrauded in business and investments and lose everything. Who can heal their bitter disappointment? Forgiveness and reconciliation can seem like a distant dream.

Yet, the victim can never be fully healed without forgiveness. The torn relationship will continue to bring pain. A bitter and unforgiving heart will only hurt the victim.

Jesus understands the danger of not forgiving others. There are at least three very good reasons for Jesus' strong stand on forgiving others. First, by reason of comparison. The debt owed to us cannot compare with the debt we owe to God. Nor can the small sacrifice I pay to forgive someone compare with the price Jesus paid.

The second reason is logic. When we ask for forgiveness we need to confess all of our sins. Over years Miroslav Volf struggled with hatred and a desire for revenge against the Serbian forces that ravaged his Croatian homeland. God taught him the important lesson about forgiving others:

We must not forget that there is an evil worse than the original crime. It consists of self-centered slothfulness of the mind, heart, and will that will not recognize one's own sinfulness, not pursue justice for the innocent, and not extend grace to the guilty.
-Miroslav Volf

A third reason we forgive others is that not forgiving can kill our heart. "Unforgiveness is the poison I drink trying to kill you." An unforgiving heart breeds grudges and bitterness – eventually killing the capacity to love. When we harbor an unforgiving heart, we rob ourselves of the release of forgiveness.

Sin is a kind of toxic waste that lasts forever if not removed by forgiveness. There was a company that tried to drill a mile-deep hole to bury toxic waste. A few years later poisonous water surfaced. PCBs contaminated the water, which seeped upwards through cracks and crevices in the underground rock.

This is how sin works. The only hope is concerted prayer as we ask for a spirit of contrition and confession – and wait for God to cleanse the soil and water of our sin.

God Gives Power And Hope To Forgive Others

For those wounded without an apology there is hope. Jesus not only died to forgive us of our sins. He gave his life to heal us of every wound we have had to suffer in a sinful and violent world:

Surely he took up our infirmities and carried our sorrows, the punishment that brought us peace was upon him, and by his wounds we are healed. (Isaiah 53:5)

This healing makes it possible for us to forgive others – from the heart. Even while you are healing, you can also take your "enemy" to Jesus in prayer. Prayer is the first and most important step in restoring relations with others:

I can no longer condemn or hate a brother for whom I pray, no matter how much trouble he causes me.
-Dietrich Bonhoeffer

Then, when your heart is ready and it is safe to do so, Jesus encourages you to go to your offender to seek reconciliation, in order to help them acknowledge their sin and move towards reconciliation.

If your brother sins against you, go and show him his fault, just between the two of you. If he listens to you, you have won your brother over. (Matthew 18:15)

This "intervention" requires wisdom and patience. We must ask for love and courage in order to be effective. We must also ask for God to open the door for the right opportunity. As he hears our prayers the hope for reconciliation becomes real.

In my own life, it took years of prayer for me to gather the courage to speak to someone who had hurt me. Fear of rejection kept me from seeing the truth – or even acknowledging my hurt and their fault. I prayed about this. Then one day we got together and God opened the door for meaningful conversation.

It went wonderfully. In fact, after willingly acknowledging his fault, this person also confronted me about my resentment and arrogance. We both felt better afterwards. We experienced reconciliation through forgiveness. Our relationship has been growing ever since.

Forgiveness Results In Relational Reconciliation

Reconciliation is the key to lasting and growing relationships with others. I think of my marriage. Caron and I have been together for over thirty years, and through many bumps and bruises our love has continually grown. The key is not compatibility or strength of character. The secret is reconciliation through forgiveness.

Saying "Sorry" and "I forgive you" improves a marriage. Parent-child relationships also grow and deepen with an honest admission of failings – on both sides.

In the workplace and public arena we experience power politics, labor strife, racial and class conflict. Without reconciliation we will destroy each other. Jesus says, "Blessed are the peacemakers." (Matthew 5:9) A Christian peacemaker is someone who prays and works for reconciliation because he has been forgiven and reconciled to God. God promises answers to our prayer:

Seek the peace and prosperity of the city to which I have carried you into exile. Pray to the Lord for it, because if it prospers, you too will prosper.
(Jeremiah 29:7)

The practice of forgiveness can be applied to every relationship – no matter how deep the problem. Broken family relationships need healing. Marriages lie in scattered shards of unresolved hurt. Friends are separated by careless words. An office team loses friendship and chemistry. A church is reduced to gossip and accusation. Fill in your own blank. Nothing is beyond the reach of Jesus.

Bring it Home

Pray It Forward:

- Pray for appointments to share with your a friend.
- Brainstorm questions specific to each of your 3 friends you are praying for.
- Brainstorm connection points to each of your friends (activities, questions, ways to serve).

Share It Outward

- **Prayer and practice steps with others:**

    1. Meet with two others (in person or by phone or online) to pray for these seeker friends. Pray for divine appointments.

    2. In response to these prayers of faith, step out boldly to share with one of your friends you are praying for to open a God conversation, to go past spirituality and purpose.

        - Ask them how they feel about talking with you about spirituality, purpose, or God. Explore. Bring up Jesus in the conversation. See what they think and feel about him.
        - Offer to pray with your friend according to their needs you know needs by now…pray beyond personal needs to God- seeking him and being thankful to him.
        - When God opens their hearts, If they are 'thirsty' and engaged, ask if they would read a book (*God in the Conversation, Reasons for God, Mere Christianity, Journey in Prayer*) and give you some feedback.

Readings:

- Read ahead and prepare Week 8.

WEEK EIGHT

Engage in Rich Spiritual Conversation with Seeking Friends

I pray that you may know what are the riches of his glorious inheritance in the saints. (Ephesians 1:18)

There are many spiritual pretenders in our world. They fill bookstores with books on enlightenment. They share their philosophies on talk shows. They make confident claims about people finding peace and balance in their inner world. They speak and write with spiritual words and phrases. They talk about an inner voice, ancient wisdom, or spontaneous awareness. If they say it with gravity or write well, they may gain a significant following.

People perceive these teachers as enlightened. That is the trick of spiritual language. Profound words seem to have meaning even when they don't. Ask the teacher to explain just what they mean by 'enlightenment' (or some other weighty word) and they speak in vague generalizations. They use words like 'consciousness,' or 'inner awareness.' They might suggest you learn to breathe in a special way, or empty your mind of conscious thought, and melt into the Oneness of all things. Underneath it all, you come to realize that for all the profound language, the words they employ are empty.

To illustrate, we do not take the term 'Infinity' seriously, when it refers to a car. The term is meant to attract purchasers and to gain admiration. It is pointless to ask a dealer what they are trying to say when they call a car 'Infinity.' We know the word has nothing to do with the car. 'Infinity' actually means nothing at all.

Certain words are common to all serious philosophical and religious thought. Four of the most important are *wisdom, revelation, enlightenment, and knowledge.* Amazingly, in the New Testament letter to the Ephesian Christians, all four words are found in one profound prayer. Far from empty syllables, each word is pregnant with meaning, rich in substance, and filled with power for this life and the next.

> *I keep asking that the God of our Lord Jesus Christ, the glorious Father, may give you the Spirit of wisdom and revelation, so that you may know him better. I pray that the eyes of your heart may be enlightened in order that you may know the hope to which he has called you.* (Ephesians 1: 19)

The apostle Paul prays to God to give Christians <sophia> 'wisdom.' They need wisdom so they can understand who Jesus is and what he does for them.

He asks God to reveal <apolcalypto> the love and character of Christ to each believer. Christ's love is the seedbed of all Christian growth. Only in the knowing of his love, can they live as children of God.

Paul prays that they may grow deeper in personal <gnosis> knowledge of Christ. This knowledge of Christ is filled with content. It is knowing his divine-human person, his sacrificial work, his character, and the truth of everything he says.

Lastly he prays that these believers may literally have an epiphany about hope. The word enlightenment comes from the Greek word <epiphanos>. Paul asks God that the Ephesians may have their eyes opened to joyfully anticipate the future God has planned for them.

Notice Paul communicates the wealth of Christian experience in a prayer. Faith is the door and prayer is the key that unlocks and accesses the treasures within. To experience these riches, we pray. To impart these blessings to others, we pray.

Wisdom, revelation, knowledge, and enlightenment are existential experiences from God – promised to each and every Christian. These deep experiences of God are part of even an 'ordinary' Christian life. There is more substance, meaning, and hope in this one prayer than in entire volumes of spiritual guidance by popular pretenders. In other words, the Christian has an inexhaustible treasure trove of genuine spiritual riches. This is what people clamour for. We have what they are looking for!

It is essential we learn to communicate our powerful experiences with God and invite others to the same amazing encounters with God that we enjoy.

Imagine saying more than "I pray when I have problems." What if you shared deeper, "When I pray, I feel God's acceptance of my prayer. I experience his presence. He tells me that my prayer matters to him. His Spirit gives me inner confidence he will answer."

Instead of merely saying, "I read the Bible to make sense of life," share, "When I read the Bible, God speaks to me, like a father to his child. He opens my heart to experience his love. He opens my eyes to understand the world around me. He reveals just what I need to know as he guides me each and every day."

Rather than generically saying, "I believe in God," go deeper, "I have had a deep experience of God. He is real to me – just as real as you are. He speaks to me and guides me. When no one else can be counted on, He never fails me, so I learn to trust and follow him."

Learn to share your experiences with Christ. Use the language that the Bible uses to help people see what is empty out there. Make your invitation rich and full with what is genuine, in contrast with the 'car lot' language of pretenders.

When you entwine your spiritual testimony with prayer- you can be sure God will use you to draw others to himself.

Scripture Study — GOING DEEP IN SPIRITUAL CONVERSATION

Read John 4: 5-30 on your own.

⁵ So he came to a town in Samaria called Sychar, near the plot of ground Jacob had given to his son Joseph. ⁶ Jacob's well was there, and Jesus, tired as he was from the journey, sat down by the well. It was about noon.

⁷ When a Samaritan woman came to draw water, Jesus said to her, "Will you give me a drink?" ⁸(His disciples had gone into the town to buy food.)

⁹ The Samaritan woman said to him, "You are a Jew and I am a Samaritan woman. How can you ask me for a drink?" (For Jews do not associate with Samaritans.)

¹⁰ Jesus answered her, "If you knew the gift of God and who it is that asks you for a drink, you would have asked him and he would have given you living water."

¹¹ "Sir," the woman said, "you have nothing to draw with and the well is deep. Where can you get this living water? ¹² Are you greater than our father Jacob, who gave us the well and drank from it himself, as did also his sons and his livestock?"

¹³ Jesus answered, "Everyone who drinks this water will be thirsty again, ¹⁴ but whoever drinks the water I give them will never thirst. Indeed, the water I give them will become in them a spring of water welling up to eternal life."

¹⁵ The woman said to him, "Sir, give me this water so that I won't get thirsty and have to keep coming here to draw water."

¹⁶ He told her, "Go, call your husband and come back."

¹⁷ "I have no husband," she replied.

Jesus said to her, "You are right when you say you have no husband. ¹⁸ The fact is, you have had five husbands, and the man you now have is not your husband. What you have just said is quite true."

¹⁹ "Sir," the woman said, "I can see that you are a prophet. ²⁰ Our ancestors worshiped on this mountain, but you Jews claim that the place where we must worship is in Jerusalem."

²¹ "Woman," Jesus replied, "believe me, a time is coming when you will worship the Father neither on this mountain nor in Jerusalem. ²² You Samaritans worship what you do not know; we worship what we do know, for salvation is from the Jews. ²³ Yet a time is coming and has now come when the true worshipers will worship the Father in the Spirit and in truth, for they are the kind of worshipers the Father seeks. ²⁴ God is spirit, and his worshipers must worship in the Spirit and in truth."

²⁵ The woman said, "I know that Messiah" (called Christ) "is coming. When he comes, he will explain everything to us."

²⁶ Then Jesus declared, "I, the one speaking to you— I am he."

²⁷ Just then his disciples returned and were surprised to find him talking with a woman. But no one asked, "What do you want?" or "Why are you talking with her?"

²⁸ Then, leaving her water jar, the woman went back to the town and said to the people, ²⁹ "Come, see a man who told me everything I ever did. Could this be the Messiah?" ³⁰ They came out of the town and made their way toward him.

How does Jesus engage this woman in conversation?

How does he go deeper?

When does he decide to bring the conversation to a decision?

PRAYER PRACTICE: In Triads, pray for someone you would like Christ to help you go deeper with.

A MODERN DAY EXAMPLE: Seven Sins on a Treadmill God in the Conversation Chapter 6:

Read the following on your own.

We are attending a workshop in downtown Toronto. I am up at first light to work out with a colleague in the hotel fitness center. Connan is on a treadmill two down from me. We engage in friendly banter.

A woman steps on the machine between us and starts her routine. It turns out she works for a city school board and is attending education meetings. Connan and I continue our conversation. Somehow we touch on the upcoming election.

She treads in and comments on the current conservative prime minister. "I just hate that Stephen Harper and his gang," she says. "They have to go."

I decide to reply. "Why?" I ask. "Surely, you don't want the other guys?"

I think I've hit a nerve. Pace quickening, pulse rising, she says, "They're out to destroy the environment. They don't do a thing about the tar sands. Big money and oil rule their decisions. They're going to ruin the world."

I get her point. According to the Pembina Institute, average greenhouse gas emissions for Alberta oil sands extraction and upgrading are estimated to be 3.2 to 4.5 times as intensive per barrel as for conventional crude oil. If Alberta were a country, at a rate of 69 tons CO_2 equivalent per person, its per capita greenhouse gas emissions would be higher than any other country in the world.

I venture a reply, "So do you think the environment is the key issue for the upcoming election?"

"Maybe it isn't the only issue. It's definitely the most important. We don't want the next generation to inherit a polluted world. Someone has to stop these guys. They just don't give a damn." She's exercised about this. Facing forward, body language tells me she's not open to debate.

I glance over at Connan. He shrugs his shoulders, "What can you say?" Connan is a good sport, always ready to discuss religion or politics, but he wonders if we haven't hit a dead end. I don't give up that easy. I figure our new exercise friend stepped into the conversation so she might be open to some friendly debate.

I try a new tack. I get an idea. A light goes on. I hope it's a prompting from God.

I take a calculated risk. I flip the question on its head.

"I agree the environment is important. Still I am pretty confident there are at least seven issues more important than the oil sands."

Connan finishes his run. He moves over to the weights. Quizzical, he looks at me, "Where are you going with this?"

She slows her pace and turns with a furrowed brow, "What are you talking about?" She looks credulous.

"Well you know – the seven things that have always been most important in any society – the heart of the whole thing."

Credulous, she says, "Go on."

For me it is 30 minutes, 3.5, kilometers and 300 calories later. I need to slow my pace and my pulse.

I pause for a minute.

The break lets her ponder where I might be headed. It also provides a breather so the conversation can cool a bit.

I try to speak calmly and matter-of-factly. "Well it's the same old seven things. You know, the big ones –wrath, greed, envy, sloth, gluttony, lust, and pride. These seven vices are a lot more serious than issues of the environment."

Maybe she appreciates the creative turn of conversation. "Okay. Tell me what you're getting at."

"When it comes to change, we have to go inside before we fix what's outside. We have to address these seven inner vices before we deal with the outer destruction of the planet."

"Hmm."

I explain, "In the middle ages, travelling theatre troupes acted out the dangers of these sins. They would personify each one, and show how they need to be kept in check before they destroy the soul. It was a powerful message. This drama was the only entertainment most people had. Remember, there was no newspapers, computers, or televisions.

"The seven deadly sins represent the pollution of our collective heart – what's inside all of us. What's inside comes first. Oil sands projects explain how we wreck the environment; greed, envy, and gluttony go a long way to explaining why. The outside is the consequence of what's going on inside. You can never fix the outside unless you work on the inside."

Stepping off the treadmill, she looks me in the eye. It isn't a friendly look, but neither is it angry. She has cooled from overheated to lukewarm.

She counters, "You say that the inside is more important than the outside. Why does the inside come first? I still think that it is criminal to neglect the environment."

I explain, "They're called the seven deadly sins for a reason. The world we live in is important. If we neglect the environment we're in big trouble. On the other hand, if we neglect our soul we're dead.

"Politicians focus on outside issues for good reasons. The heart is harder to change than the environment. They want to tackle the outside issues and make them the big deal. We ignore the ecosystem of our heart and inner motive. We focus on externals in order to distract us from dealing with inside issues. We don't want to be wrong. We don't want to go inside. That means, the inner pollution never gets cleaned up. It just accumulates until the arteries of our spiritual heart are hopelessly clogged."

She ponders for a minute, then replies, "I have to admit that's an interesting perspective."

"A polluted environment is the result of a bunch of polluted hearts. You can't just tell people to start treating the world with respect. You can try to vote and legislate clean air and water into the world but it won't last. Clean up the heart, and you'll clean up the world."

She has cooled down. She doesn't say anything. I can tell she is pondering what I am saying. She could be looking at her own heart.

I decide to go deeper. "Jesus says something interesting to the politicians of his time, "You always clean the outside of the cup and neglect the inside.' Then he tells them, 'First clean the inside of the cup, and then clean the outside.'

We step off the treadmill within a few minutes of each other, me first.

We finish our exercise and our conversation at the same time. We have had a good workout in more ways than one.

She has a smile. "I have to admit, you have an interesting perspective."

Cool down period is over. So is our talk.

Discuss in groups of three.

How does the conversation get going?

Why did the woman continue to listen?

Write down a few ideas of how to bring God into the conversation with your friend you just prayed for.

PRAYER PRACTICE: Share your ideas and then pray for one another's friend.

OPEN THE DOOR TO PRAYER BY GOING DEEPER INTO A GOD CONVERSATION

1. Ask diagnostic and exploratory questions that bridge to prayer and spirituality.

- Example Question: "What do you think the difference is between prayer & meditation?" Give them time to ponder.

- If they answer, "I am not sure," reply with a Question: "Would you say prayer is more about God and meditation is more about inner peace?"

- There are lots of possibilities here, but most will offer a suggestion.

2. Explore their answer with active listening and curiosity

- Example Question: Do you have any spiritual practices – like meditation, yoga, or prayer?
  Answer: No... then see where this goes....

- If Yes... then see where this goes

- Question: Are you a part of any study or group or church to grow in your spirituality?

3. Share your prayer story and go deeper

- If you reach a point in the conversation where they are engaging in the topic with interest, share something about your own spiritual practices as a springboard to invite them to explore the topic more personally. For example, "My spiritual practice is prayer. Would you be interested in hearing how I am growing in my prayer life?"

4. If God opens their heart and they are listening attentively and asking questions...

- Share how you encounter Jesus in prayer. Ask if they would like to pray. Ask if they would to learn how. Offer to teach them the Lord's Prayer. Journey in Prayer with Jesus is designed specifically for seekers to learn how to pray the way Jesus taught.

In groups of three, take turns role playing. One can be a Christian who facilitates the questions while others act as sincere seekers in response. Write your replies here:

What do you think is the difference between prayer and meditation?

Do you have any spiritual practices - like meditation, yoga or prayer?

"My spiritual practice is prayer. Would you be interested in hearing how I am growing in my prayer life?

PRAYER PRACTICE:

Share with one another about a seeker friend you are praying for. Now pray for each other to have an open door to share it with a friend.

Prayer Friendship Skill

PREPARE YOUR PRAYER TESTIMONY

Use the following questions as a starting point in sharing your experience of prayer. You do not need to answer every question; these are simply a spring board.

Begin by praying and asking the Holy Spirit to guide you.

BEFORE YOU DISCOVERED PRAYER FRIENDSHIP

1. What was your view or practice of prayer before you became a Christian?

2. What role did prayer play in how you became a Christian? What role does it play in your faith?

3. How did you begin to pray? What led you to explore? What were you hoping would happen?

SPELLING OUT YOUR PRAYER TESTIMONY

4. What motivates you to pray?

5. What difference does prayer make in your life?

6. How are you growing in prayer friendship with God now?

7. What scriptures have guided your prayers in a meaningful way?

8. What happens/changes as you pray? How do you feel before, during, after prayer?

9. Describe what prayer is to a seeker friend? What is Jesus' role in it?

Helpful Hints

Consider these suggestions for how you might share your "prayer stories" and experiences in a way that is helpful to seekers.

1. Focus on your friendship with God through Jesus, and on the relational aspects of prayer, on the things happening at the heart/spiritual level. Limit emphasis on external rituals or reli- gious practices.

2. Share your overall process of prayer growth, with specific and appropriate examples of an- swered prayer or transformation you have experienced in prayer.

3. Find connection points or themes that non-Christians can relate to. Be aware of "Chris- tianese" or "insider church language. Define any religious or theological terms you use. Write the way you speak. Keep the tone conversational.

4. Share your prayer testimony draft with both Christians and non-Christians asking for their feedback of clarity. Try practicing it to become more natural and comfortable with it.

5. Pray for opportunities to share it with others.

EXAMPLES of things I might say, and passages that inspire me. God hears me and answers me when I pray

- *God carries me through, and lifts my heart when I am down. He helps me keep on keeping on.*

- *God shows me a path forward. He gives me light to see. Things become clear.*

- *God gives me hope and courage when I feel hopeless. He fills me with strength when I feel weak.*

"Having the eyes of your hearts enlightened, that you may know what is the hope to which he has called you, what are the riches of his glorious inheritance in the saints, and what is the immeasurable greatness of his power toward us who believe… May you be strengthened with all power, according to his glorious might, for all endurance and patience with joy, giving thanks to the Father. (Ephesians 1:18-19, Colossians 1:11,12)

Here is what it feels like when I connect with God in prayer

- *He reveals himself to me and helps me realize I am his child, that Christ loves me.*

- *He tells me it is 'okay'… that he is with me.*

- *He fills me with himself.*

Ephesians 3… *For this reason I bow my knees before the Father, 15 from whom every family in heaven and on earth is named, 16 that according to the riches of his glory he may grant you to be strengthened with power through his Spirit in your inner being, 17 so that Christ may dwell in your hearts through faith—that you, being rooted and grounded in love, 18 may have strength to comprehend with all the saints what is the breadth and length and height and depth, 19 and to know the love of Christ that surpasses knowledge, that you may be filled with all the fullness of God.*

The experience when we pray in groups of people who love to pray.

- *We feel and experience how Jesus is really close. Prayer becomes easy and enjoyable.*

- *We get answers to our prayers. It makes us open our eyes and be thankful.*

Matthew 18: *19 Again I say to you, if two of you agree on earth about anything they ask, it will be done for them by my Father in heaven. 20 For where two or three are gathered in my name, there am I among them."*

PRAYER TESTIMONY SAMPLES

I have been a Christian for many years. I went to Catholic school and have known Jesus since I was a teenager. I became a Christian when I was 18. When someone becomes a Christian, they have to answer a very important question which is "Do you accept Jesus Christ as your personal savior?" Although I answered yes to this question I couldn't honestly say that he was my personal saviour. It was because, for a long time, my relationship with Jesus was not very personal. He was more a 'cosmic' saviour then a personal savior to me. I was grateful to Jesus. Therefore, I tried hard to obey God because I felt in debt to Jesus and I have a duty to obey. Out of gratitude and out of guilt I tried to be a 'good' Christian. I couldn't help but still feel condemned whenever I sinned.

I also prayed but prayer was not part of my life. I prayed because that is what Christians do. So I followed others' examples and I prayed before meals and I prayed with other Christians at church meetings. I cared for my friends. So whenever I was asked I willingly prayed for their needs to be met and problems to be resolved. But I often doubted if God was actually listening or if he will answer me.

Six years ago I moved to Vancouver with my wife. In my search for a new job, God led me to work for Prayer Current – a prayer discipleship ministry. At the time, I seriously questioned God about this new 'assignment' as prayer was not even 'my thing'. Little did I know that the assignment was all for my own benefits. I had much to learn and grow in my prayer life.

I was trained to pray at Prayer Current. We prayed on all occasions. It felt awkward and artificial at first. But slowly prayer became natural and a part of my life. It closed the loop from my brain to my heart. For years I have heard and read about Jesus, but not until I started talking to him about my feelings and struggles did Jesus become a person and a friend. Prayer became my natural response when I am reading the Bible or when I am listening to a sermon. I learned to surrender to God and ask him to change me as I pray.

"For through the law I died to the law so that I might live for God. I have been crucified with Christ and I no longer live, but Christ lives in me." – Galatians 2:19-20

Over time, Jesus and his grace become real. Now, I pray to confess because it gives me power to overcome. I pray to praise God because I love and revere him. I still pray for my friends' needs but mostly I pray that they will meet Jesus - my friend and my personal savior.

Prayer is a natural reaction for every human being. Just look at how we react to personal difficulty, "Where are you God?" or "God, help!" Or when a natural disaster strikes, the world responds, "My thoughts and prayers go out to [place]."

I'm no different in praying in crisis. Conflicts, cross road decisions, or needing money – here I recognize I'm not really at all in control of my life. I see my obvious for a power outside of myself, for God to intervene.

In prayer, we can bring everything to God. Prayer is personal first hand communication with God. It's a miracle gift, given how we break relationship with God all the time by going our own way. Our relationship with God is made possible by his son Jesus' unbroken relationship with him — that was broken when he died on the cross, to exchange and restore our broken relationship with God. Jesus brings us to God.

Earlier in my spiritual journey, I treated prayer as a pragmatic means to get things from God, seeing him as a genie magically solving my problems. These days, I'm growing in experiencing prayer more as friendship with God, talking with him honestly about everything.

"Do not be anxious about anything, but in every situation, by prayer and petition, with thanksgiving, present your requests to God. And the peace of God, which transcends all understanding, will guard your hearts and your minds in Christ Jesus."
~Philippians 4:6-7

Recently I wanted a certain outcome in a challenging relationship. I started with "anxious prayer" focusing on the problem, instead of conversing with God. I tried to analyze and predict what the other person might think or do, and calculate my actions to try to sway them.

Eventually I exhausted myself with the burden of trying to solve things on my own. I heard Jesus inviting me to let him carry it. As I turned to my attention to God, he gave me an assurance of his love, and that he knew my heart and the other person's. He reminded me of his power and wisdom, how He ultimately holds the future.

In prayer, my heart settled down. I gradually let go of fear and the need for control and certainty. I felt freedom to accept the other person and the situation no matter how it worked out, even if nothing changed. While I asked God for the outcome I desired, I also surrendered to whatever God's good will was.

In prayer, Jesus took the burden and replaced my anxiety with peace and anticipation to see where God would work.

In this situation and all of life, engaging in a dynamic prayer friendship with God changes me. He changes my heart, my view of God, how I perceive myself. This in turn changes how I see and engage with people and the world around me.

Readings

OUTWARDLY WASTING, INWARDLY RENEWING

Chapter 12 from *God in the Conversation*

It's near the end. I hold Ted's hand and pray with him. I recite verses from the Psalms and the words of Jesus. He is silent, forcing a smile with his eyes. Only his eyes have any light left. Everything else is dark. Emaciated from cancer, Ted is resigned to the outcome. When I first met him, he was about 5'8" and 180 pounds. Now, three years later, Ted is less than 100 pounds. Outwardly he has wasted away, inwardly he is renewed, at the threshold of a new life.

With affectionate memories, I look back on the several conversations of our three-year friendship.

***

I meet Ted in November 2008 after we move into our summer cottage in Okanagan Center. He runs the corner store. I retreat to the cottage a few days every month or so – mostly during the winter. My life is busy and a regular time alone is something to which I really look forward. Every few days I walk over to the store to get basics.

I notice Ted doesn't look healthy. He is only in his mid-fifties, but his skin is ashen-grey. He is shy but friendly. We always exchange small talk.

Ted lives alone. He doesn't get much business in the winter. Most people just drop by to pick up milk or eggs and say hi. One day I stop by. Ted is sitting in front of a TV screen. The light is low. He is watching a hockey game.

He looks a little rumpled and sad. I think this is normal for Ted. Old hurts are written on his eyes and never really go away, until the last few weeks of his life.

I ask "Hey Ted, would you like some company. I like to watch hockey."

"Sure" he says.

This becomes our habit for the next two winters. We both enjoy hockey. We banter about who deserves to win or lose, who will score the most goals, and how we're frustrated when our favorite team can't seem to get traction.

***

Some eighteen months before the end, I come by the store. There are no customers. Ted looks downhearted, even more than usual. His eyes are heavy and dark. I ask if everything is okay.

"I just found out I have cancer. It looks pretty bad." Ted says this in a matter of fact way, but I hear the fear. I feel the aloneness.

"Oh no. Tell me it's not true, Ted. I'm so sorry."

"I go in next week to find out about treatment."

"That's hard."

"Yeah."

"Do you want to talk about it?"

"No. I don't think so, but thanks."

"Well I'll be praying for you. You can count on that." This might be a first for Ted. He looks quizzical, and appreciative at the same time. After a pause, he says, "I would like that."

Feeling the weight of the moment. I take a small risk. "I don't want to be seem presumptuous Ted, but would you mind if I say a brief prayer for you now?"

Pause. "Well, okay... sure."

I pray a simple prayer, something like this: "Father, I pray for Ted. I'm sorry to hear of his cancer. I know it is hard. I pray that you'll be with Ted to help him through this. Give him courage. Grant him healing. We will thank you for your help. I pray in Jesus' name."

"Thanks John. I appreciate that."

This becomes the first of many times I pray with Ted.

***

Some weeks later, I drop by and Ted is watching hockey again. He likes Toronto. I like Calgary. His team is playing. He is happy for me to sit and join him.

I know Ted is wrestling with life and death. Like all of us, when he wakes in the middle of the night, he has to face the demons alone.

As we get talking, Ted lets me into his past. He tells me that he is estranged from his family and seldom sees his children. This is the 'other hurt' in his life. As a wise king Solomon put it, "The heart knows its own bitterness."

Ted is a private person. He changes topics. "I started treatments this week. I'll be doing this for the next three or four months, and then they'll decide if I need radiation."

ENGAGE THE CONVERSATION with God, with believers, with seekers

"That has to be pretty scary."
He looks at me, "Yeah. Well. I guess… Yeah it is."

Ted explains the regimen to me. After treatments, they send him home with pills that are part of his treatment. I know he will be given painkillers at some point. At first he doesn't want them.

I offer to pray for him again.

This time his response is less cautious. "I'd like that."

This time I pray a little longer. I go a little deeper. I put my hand on his shoulder.

I pray something like this: "Father, I bring Ted before you. He is facing some deep sorrows and tough trials. I pray you would give him courage and help him conquer his fears. I pray you will do the same for me – when I am overcome by my fears. I recall the psalm that says, 'I cried out to the Lord and he delivered me from all my fears.' Help us as we cry out to you."

I pause for a minute before continuing, "I pray that you will grant healing and courage to Ted – healing to his body and courage for his soul. Give the doctors wisdom and bless the treatments. We know that You are our healer, and that You can do all things. I pray especially you will help Ted to give his cares and his fears to you.' I pause for a minute to give Ted a chance to silently pray if he feels like it. I end, "And because Jesus knows all about our sorrow and pain, I ask this in Jesus' name."

I hear a heavy sigh. I feel his shoulders rise and fall. A prayer goes deeper than any other words. Prayer brings God into the conversation.

***

A few months later I visit the store. Ted's weight loss is visible. His face is thinner. A belt is drawn tight over sagging pants that are now way too big. We have a good visit. I ask about his family, whether they know how he is doing and when they might visit. He tells me about a divorce that went sour and about kids and grandkids he used to see all the time. He doesn't show a lot of emotion but I know this is the central hurt of his life. Even the cancer doesn't go as deep. Maybe this explains his silent retreat from the world.

I offer to pray. This time, Ted has been waiting for me to offer. His body is hurting and his spirit is heavy. I put my hand on his shoulder. We both bow our heads. I pray a longer prayer, and add some of the Bible passages I am familiar with, especially the Psalm 23. This psalm of David is a light in dark times for those who suffer.

"The Lord is my Shepherd, I shall not want.
He makes me to lie down in green pastures.
He leads me beside the still waters. He restores my soul.
He leads me in paths of righteousness for his names sake
Yea though I walk through the valley of the shadow of death I will fear no evil.
You are with me. Your rod and your staff comfort me."

***

The next time we have an extended visit is a few months later. It's late spring. Flowers are beginning to open and trees are budding. Everything is coming to life. The lake shimmers with light. Inside the store is a different matter. There's no hint of spring. The light is dim. Ted is worse for wear. He's lost about 25 pounds. This is an aggressive cancer, maybe stage 4. I don't ask.

Ted's decay has spread to the store. Entering, a person can feel his exhaustion. It sits heavy on the place. Ted used to keep everything ship-shape. Now the shelves are barely stocked. DVDs are scattered on the counter behind the cash register. The fridges have a build up of ice. His desk is a mess – littered with bills and records.

Ted is sitting on his favorite chair. I sit next to him. We don't chitchat so much any more. After greetings and touching base, I ask Ted about his experience with God and religion.

"I used to pray. I don't much anymore."

"Tell me about it."

He seems reluctant but willing at the same time. I think he knows he needs to discuss his past. "My wife became a Jehovah's Witness. This is how we brought up our family. I used to read the books, say the prayers and practice the religion."

"Really? What happened?"

"Well my wife and I grew apart and we got divorced. That was the same time I stopped my involvement with the Witnesses and pretty much stopped praying."

Ted didn't seem to want to say anymore about his private life. It's hard for him. He makes a reference to 'strict religion.'

I offer to pray. Ted says "Sure. Please. I would appreciate it."

Before I do, I ask "Ted would you like to pray along with me?"

"I'm not sure."

"How about saying the words after I say them? That might make it easier – just a way to help out."

"Well maybe."

"Let me start and then you can try if you feel like it."

I begin, "Dear Father, thank you for being kind and merciful..."

I wait through an awkward silence. After a generous pause, I assume Ted doesn't want to pray out loud. I am about to continue, and then I hear him, his voice quiet and halting, "Dear Father, thank you for being kind and merciful..."

I keep the prayer short. I recite a few Bible verses from the gospels. Ted repeats them. I continue, "But thank you for the good news that you are the resurrection and the life." I add a few other short sentences. Ted repeats phrase after phrase.

Then I finish, "And we pray in Jesus' name. Amen." Ted takes his time on this one. A Jehovah's Witness does not pray to Jesus. He waits a second – and then says, "And we pray in Jesus' name. Amen."

Before I go I say, "Hey Ted, I'm glad we could pray together. Thanks for the privilege."

***

The next time we meet, we both pray again. After we pray, I ask, "Ted, do you find it helpful when I quote Bible verses when we pray?"

"Yes, I do."

"Would you like me to write down some passages that have been a great comfort to me? You can look at them when you feel down or worried. You can recite the passages to God like a prayer."

"Sure. Okay. That might be good."

Before I head back to Vancouver, I write out a dozen or so of my favorite courage and hope passages. I have memorized several for my own times of need:

> *"I cried out to the Lord and he heard me and delivered me from all my fears." (Psalm 34:4)*
>
> *"Jesus said, 'I am the resurrection and the life. He who believes in me will never die.'" (John 11:17)*
>
> *"So we do not lose heart. Though our outer self is wasting away, our inner self is being renewed day by day.". (2 Corinthians 4:16)*

I sense his deep need. I feel the fear that crouches, ready to pounce. I start praying for him pretty much each day. I ask others to pray for him too.

***

Time passes. It's now the fall of his last year. The trees have turned brown. The vines are empty. The lake is dark and still. Ted has dwindled to a skeleton. The skin seems to hang on his frame. His eyes are gaunt. He weighs no more than 120 pounds. The disease has taken over. Whatever the chemo is doing, Ted is getting worse. He is going to die, and it won't be long. Ted never complains. Now he's getting radiation treatments and he takes a regular dose of morphine for the pain.

After a few friendly words, I start our times by reading a few passages of Scripture and explain the comfort in them. Then we pray together.

At some point, I bring him a Bible with special passages bookmarked. It is a user-friendly version in today's English. I put a plastic sticky tab in maybe 30 places. I mark several Psalms, key sayings of Jesus, and several passages in the rest of the New Testament that are laced with comfort and hope of eternal life. He says he will read them.

Some passages are just praise and thanksgiving. I explain to Ted that worshipping God is a great way to take his mind off his own troubles and pain. I take time to go through various passages, and explain how he can use the words of God to navigate his pain and trials. We keep going back to Paul's words in the letter to the Corinthians: *"Outwardly we are wasting away, but inwardly we are being renewed day by day."* (2 Corinthians 4:16)

I try to help Ted understand that this world is not all that there is. A better world waits. Our decaying bodies will die, but we will live. Every believer will trade in his old perishing body and get a new one.

I gradually notice a change – not the changes caused by cancer. I begin to see a light in Ted's eyes. It is a glimmer of hope.

***

Some weeks later we meet again. Winter has set in. Ted is down to 100 pounds. He knows he's going to die. I know he's going to die.

We still pray for his healing but now I want to help him get ready to die.

"Ted you do not seem to be getting better. Tell me how things are going."

He is seated behind his old desk, hunched over, as usual.

He looks up at me. "Not good," he admits.

"You know I hope and pray you will beat this – but I need to ask. Are you ready to face dying?"

I can see Ted dreads this turn of conversation. I can also see he is relieved to talk about it.

While he searches for words, I decide to continue, "I want you to live but I also want to comfort you and give you courage to face the worst if it happens. Can we try to do that?"

"Okay. What do you mean?"

"I want you to know that Jesus can take you through anything – even death."

Ted looks at me, inviting me to continue.

"Let me read for you about a powerful event in the life of Jesus. It comes from the gospel of John. Try to put yourself in the picture and to feel the hope."

"There is this man called Lazarus. He dies. Everyone is weeping and mourning in a loud open way – crying and weeping."

I start to read from the gospel of John, chapter 11:

Lazarus' sister, Martha, says to Jesus, "Rabbi, if you had been here Lazarus would not have died."

Jesus asks her, "Do you believe this?"

Martha says, "Yes. I believe you are the Messiah, sent from God."

Jesus says to her, "Your brother will rise again." Martha said to him, "I know that he will rise again in the resurrection on the last day." Jesus said to her, "I am the resurrection and the life. Whoever believes in me, though he die, yet shall he live, and everyone who lives and believes in me shall never die. Do you believe this?" She said to him, "Yes, Lord; I believe that you are the Christ, the Son of God, who is coming into the world."

At this point Jesus heads over to the cave Lazarus is buried in. He cries out with a loud voice, "Lazarus come out!" Out walks Lazarus, still wrapped in his grave cloths."

I ask Ted, "Are you familiar with the story?"

"I think I read it once."

"Jesus is talking to you and to me here Ted. If you believe in Christ you will be raised from the dead and will live forever with him. Your outer body is wasting away – but inside you can get stronger every day. One day you will get a new body that is perfect and ageless and filled with joy. The life Jesus is talking about begins today – here and now. What do you think – do you believe this?"

Ted looks up at me. "I want to. I'm not sure."

"How about if we pray? God can help you believe if you ask him. I am going to pray for you and you can say the prayer after me if you want."

Ted nods, "Okay."

I pray a prayer one phrase at a time. Ted quietly whispers each phrase.

"Father, we are suffering here... This body is wasting away with this cancer... We know you can give new life even now... and that we can experience the resurrection Jesus is talking about here... Our faith is weak... We need help to believe in you... to believe that you can forgive us of all our sins and give us eternal life... Please strengthen our faith so we can believe. In Jesus' name we pray, Amen."

Ted says, "Thanks John. I mean it. This helps."

Through winter and spring I see Ted several more times. I leave him with a CD of worship songs. He comes to deeply enjoy them. The choir has some six different nationalities represented. The music is stirring and rich.

As the cancer progresses Ted fades away. He takes oral treatment, radiation, and increased morphine. I check in on him regularly. I pray with him and ask if the Bible passages help him. At first he reads the passages and tells me they are helpful. I notice he still has a 'New World' translation – the Jehovah's Witness version, beside him.

As time and cancer progress, Ted stops reading. He takes a stronger dose of morphine. He says, "I can't concentrate to read, but I still listen to the music you gave me. It really gives me strength."

We continue our talks, prayers and Bible reading each time we meet. I add words from some great hymns, like "Holy Holy Holy," "Rock of Ages," and "Great is Thy Faithfulness." Ted is glad for this. He always says, "Thanks John, for coming by. It means a lot to me."

***

Summer arrives and we are on family vacation. As it turns out, our vacation and Ted's passing intersect. As I look back, I thank God for this. It is no coincidence.

I drop by the store, which is now being run by Ted's friend. Ted is upstairs.

I climb the steps and walk into his bedroom. There is a strong smell and I notice alarming stains on the carpet. Ted has lost bowel control and is now bleeding internally. I find him curled up – a heap of bones and skin. He is wasting away, living one breath at a time.

I sit by him. He wakes for a minute. I want to care for him and comfort him in some way. "Hey Ted. It's rough isn't it? I know it can't get any harder." He can hardly whisper. He just nods. I get him water. He sips through parched cracked lips. I'm deeply moved. I think I am feeling what God is feeling – I'm sharing the heart of God for one of his children. Words are helpful but he also needs touch – like a crying child.

I put my hand on his shoulder. He groans quietly. I feel his humiliation and pain. I put my hand on his head and gently stroke it. He quietly lets me. I do this for a few minutes. I remind him of a few of our favorite passages. I recite one after another from memory.

> *"Outwardly we are wasting away, but inwardly we are being renewed day by day...God is preparing us for an eternal weight of glory." (2 Corinthians 4:16-17)*
>
> *"Eye has not seen nor has ear heard nor has the mind of man conceived what God has prepared for those he loves and who are called according to his purpose." (1 Corinthians 2:9)*

"Isn't this good news Ted? It won't be long now. Soon there will be peace and rest – a whole new life without any sorrow or disease."

"Yes. Yes."

"You believe this don't you Ted? "Yes." He cringes with pain, "Yes. I do."

I want to comfort him any way I can. I'm not a good singer. Normally I would call my singing painful, but I feel compelled. I sing the words of the "The Lord is my shepherd"... I sing another hymn I have memorized, "Rock of Ages, cleft for me." Ted silently lets it soak in to his weary and broken body. I just sit beside him – until he falls asleep.

***

A few days later I find out Ted's family is visiting. His two daughters have kids. Their visit represents forgetting the past. They want to see their dad and granddad and tell him they love him.

After a few days with Ted, they come over to ask me if I would be willing to plan a memorial for after their dad dies.

"Of course. It would be an honor."

I share a few words of hope with his daughters. I tell them how Ted and I have been getting to know each other. I share how Ted has been getting to know God. I tell them how special it has been to be with Ted and what a privilege it has been to pray with him. They have a good cry.

It turns out there are too many relatives to stay in Ted's home. We have room and private space they can enjoy as a family. As it turns out, they take us up on the offer and stay with us the days before Ted passes and then leading up to the service.

I drop by a few more times in the next week to comfort Ted and pray with him.

***

One morning I find out Ted has gone to hospice care in Kelowna. I go to visit. I find Ted lying in his bed. He is unconscious from all the pain and medication. His two daughters and their children are in the room waiting for the end. They tell me how they had a chance to say goodbye and to hug and cry with their dad.

I sit by Ted. I stroke his head. I quietly say a prayer – filled with comfort and hope from the scriptures. I tell him how thankful I am for our friendship and how glad I am we will meet again in a better world.

After a while I leave the family to be alone with their dad. This is the last time I will see Ted. His life has come full circle. I find out the next day, Ted has passed away.

***

A few days later the whole community gathers to say goodbye to Ted. I know my role. It's my part to help people remember Ted, and maybe let them see a side of him they didn't know.

While people are finding seats, the CD I gave to Ted plays in the background. At the service a daughter and granddaughter share cherished memories of Ted. A neighbor does as well.

When it's my turn, I narrate recent conversations and prayers with Ted. I read some of his favorite passages. I talk about our times of prayer together. From the CD, we play one of the songs, which Ted grew to love. I share how he grew stronger in faith and soul even while his body wasted away.

It is a rich time. There is a warm glow in the room. We all have a chance to remember Ted, and get to know him a little better. There is so much hope. I don't think anyone leaves depressed. There is even a hint of celebration as we all think about Ted's hope for a new life.

Bring it Home

Pray it forward:

- Pray, asking "How can I bring God into the conversation with my seeker friends?"
- Review and complete your prayer story.

Prayer and practice steps with others:

1. Meet with your triad. Continue praying for each other and friends.

    - Thank God for answers! Progress!
    - Share with each other and give feedback on your testimony – on how it might connect with a non-Christian.

2. Make an appointment with a friend. If God opens the door, seek to go deeper in conversation with them (see above). If things go well share your prayer testimony with them. Let them know how you feel about God! As God gives openness, ask if they would like to learn how to prayffe. Offer to teach them how to pray.

Readings:

- Read ahead and prepare Week 9.

WEEK NINE

Pray With and Teach Seeking Friends How to Pray

Teach a friend to pray, and you will introduce them to Jesus

Teaching someone to pray is a privilege which can emerge from a genuine friendship. . It can also create a friendship. I can think of no greater gift to impart to someone than to teach them to pray. If they receive this gift they can dive in and navigate life with God on their own. Until they have this gift they remain on the outside of his joy and friendship.

Prayer evangelism is not a technique. It is about building solid and caring relationships with others – whether Christians or non-Christians. The important thing is to combine relationship building with open and honest communication about your faith. Get to know them. Make a friend. The stronger the bridge of friendship, the greater the opportunity to bring a friend to Jesus through teaching them to pray.

I recall meeting a single mother who makes friends easily. When others are struck by her positive and hopeful manner, they ask her, "How do you manage to do it?" She replies, "I pray." This makes her friends think – and often leads to some kind of God conversation. It is not about 'laying your trip' on someone; it is about sharing your prayer experience with Jesus.

There is a wide open door of opportunity to teach people about prayer today. We might assume that people are reluctant or closed when it comes to learning how to pray. Actually, most people I meet are curious about prayer. In a 2016 Angus Reid Canada-wide survey on prayer, 40% of Canadians pray frequently, 45% occasionally, and 85% overall. They might be shy to bring up the topic, yet once it is brought into the conversation, they are often open and willing to learn more.

In the movie *Gravity*, Sandra Bullock's character is an astronaut entering the atmosphere from outer space. She is going too fast and thinks she is done for. She says, "I guess I should pray." After a moment she reflects, "But I don't know how." Another pause, and then, "No one ever taught me." I have found that many people today are in the same state – they would like to know how to pray but no one ever taught them.

There is a sequence to prayer evangelism. It is a friendship sequence.

First we pray for our friend on our own. We talk to God about our friend before we talk to our friend about God.

Next, in response to a tangible need, we pray for them in their presence. If you hear a great sorrow or joy you can ask, "Can I pray for you about this?" For example, my friend has survived the loss of a child and cancer. One day she walked by our home. She looked so sad. I had to try to comfort her. I have prayed with her a few times before. When she shared her current sorrow, I asked if I could pray for her. In prayer I quoted the words of Jesus, "Come unto me you that labor and are heavy laden, and I will give you rest. Take my yoke upon you and learn from me, for I am meek and lowly and you will find rest for your souls." She looked at me with a sad smile. "John, I have tried church and religion so many times. It just doesn't work for me." I replied, "That's okay. For now just try Jesus."

As you pray a right time will come when God opens them to listen to you. Ask them if they would like to pray as well. If they are willing, they can say a prayer in their own words. If they are uncomfortable praying on their own, you can say "Prayer is not complicated. You can repeat after me."

At this point, you can ask if they would like to learn how to pray- or they might ask you to teach them to pray. If not, you can offer them to read *Journey in Prayer* or some other helpful introductory or basic book on prayer.

Praying with someone is the best form of friendship communication. Recently, one woman shared with me how her brother phoned from his home overseas to say. "My wife and I are getting a divorce".. Instead of scolding, she simply responded, "I know how much you are hurting. Can I pray for you now?"

After a moment of silence, he said "Yes." She prayed a lengthy and grace-filled prayer for her brother." God ministered. He was deeply moved. They grew closer to God and closer to each other.

When we pray for someone, we bring God into the conversation. When we pray with someone this becomes close and personal. When we help someone pray, we bring them into conversation with God. When they know how to pray, they are already on the path to knowing Jesus and becoming his friend.

Praying for and with someone is a part of loving them; it is a tangible expression of care for them no matter where they are in their spiritual journey. After I shared about prayer friendship a woman approached me. She spoke with a breaking voice. She said, "I am a nurse. I have been at the bedside of many dying patients. I never prayed with them. How I wish I had thought of this before, and simply taken their hand and offered up a prayer with them."

When we pray, we bring God into the conversation. He shows up! When we pray using his Word, we minister the message to the one we pray with. It is a kind way to preach the good news.

THE PROGRESS OF PRAYER EVANGELISM

1. **Pray for appointments.**
2. **Pray for someone.**
3. **Pray with someone. Invite them to offer up a prayer.**
4. **Offer to teach them to pray.**

Scripture Study

On your own, spend time writing down a few favorite passages that have helped and comforted you. Spend some time praying them.

In your group: now take some time to share these passages with your group.

PRAYER PRACTICE: Practice praying these passages for one another.

Prayer Friendship Skill
PRAY JESUS' KINGDOM PRAYER APPLIED TO SEEKERS

I need a job. I need money to pay the bills.
My famiy member who has cancer. They need healing.
I need to make the right decision at a crossroads.
Pray for my exams, that I might do well.

Sound familiar? These are some of the most common and tangible prayer needs, among believers and non-Christians alike. So often we are quick to pray in times of crisis. Whether it is an individual feeling stress at a life circumstance, or whether it is the world "offering their prayers and thoughts" after a natural disaster strikes, crises prompt us to pray. In these times, we more acutely recognize our weakness, and our need for help outside of ourselves.

While we can be free in bringing our every need to our Father God in prayer, how can we deepen or expand our prayer focus beyond mere survival of hardship or removal of problems? How can we pray for these earthly challenges in a way that is kingdom-centred and Christ-empowered?

A helpful approach is to use the Lord's prayer as a lens to pray through a petition or prayer challenge, with a kingdom perspective. Let the Holy Spirit guide you in how each line of the prayer applies to the specific situation you are interceding for.

Testimony of Praying the Lord's Prayer with a Seeker

I had heard my roommate crying in her room for several weeks. Eventually she opened up. She was at an impasse with her immigration situation. She was in an exploitative employment situation due to her lack of status, not wanting to give her boss any reason to fire her and give up the sponsorship process for her papers.

I offered to pray with her. "Father, thank you that you are a good Father that loves her so much. Reveal your love to her in this situation, especially wherever she may be struggling with doubt. Holy is your name. Show her more of who you are, and how you are good and holy in how you work. Let your kingdom come and your will be done. She has desired her immigration dream so much. Help her to surrender to whatever you plans are, that she might grow in trusting you and your plans. Give her daily bread. Provide her the strength, faith, and finances to walk through this. Forgive her if she has any ill feeling toward her boss. May she be gracious in her interactions at work. Lead her and guide her, and pen up a new way where there seems to be no way. Deliver her from discouragement or despair. Fill her with hope, that she would see and experience you in new ways.

Shortly after, she emailed me. "I want to thank you for praying for me. It is a very kind gesture from you to include me in your prayers. It is very hard for me to open up with someone and tell my problems, maybe because I feel more vulnerable. But as you said, sometimes we have to give up and accept that we need help of any kind and having you praying is a blessing. I believe prayers are very powerful. You can instantly see a change. If things don't change, at least your soul feels in peace. And that's exactly how I felt after I left your room that night. The next day at work, someone recommended a lawyer who specializes in cases like mine who has a very high success rate. That was an answer to what you prayed for, a new path that I couldn't see before. Thank you again."

Identify a practical prayer need in the life of your focus group of seeker friends.

Write a prayer out following the framework of the Lord's prayer.

"Father, hallowed be your name.

Your kingdom come.

Give us each day our daily bread,

and forgive us our sins,

 for we ourselves forgive everyone who is indebted to us.

And lead us not into temptation."

Readings

SHE LEARNS TO HAVE CONVERSATIONS WITH GOD THROUGH HELL AND HIGH WATER

Chapter 11 from *God in the Conversation*

Since she was a little girl, Susan has prayed every day. No one has taught her how. She prays for her friends, loved ones, and people in need – pretty much the whole world. She attends church occasionally – more in recent years.

I know Sue well. We're good friends. She's also my sister.

During a difficult, no, a horrendous year of her life, she invites me to teach her how to pray.

When our training starts, Sue is battling breast cancer. She has her meltdowns but she's a fighter who doesn't know the word 'quit.' A vast team of friends and family rally around her. They raise a ton of money for cancer research. Sue has the ability to rally people to a good cause. Even with a full time job she finds time to volunteer for the national director position of Ronald MacDonald House.

I pray with her over the phone. I ask God to heal her body and to strengthen her soul. She loves that.

***

One day at the family summer cottage we get talking. I ask her, "Would you like to learn more about prayer? I'd be happy to come alongside and help." Some years earlier she read a book called "Seven Days of Prayer with Jesus." It's about Jesus' prayer. She found it encouraging.

"I would love that, John."

We sit beside each other in a well-lit corner. The sunlight streams across the deck. We face a sylvan lake. It's a beautiful summer day.

We talk about the suffering and pain and get talking about prayer. I ask her, "Why does Jesus encourage us to call God 'Our Father'?"

"Well God loves us and takes care of us, right?"

"Did you know that God has more than a hundred names in the Bible, but Jesus uses only one. He calls God 'Father' every time. The one exception – on the cross he cries 'My God my God why have you forsaken me?' Why do you think that is?"

"Well God must want us to think of him in a very personal way."

"Right. God is not just an 'anybody' God. He's a personal God. He's our Father because he created us. He becomes our Father, in the deepest sense, as we trust him for everything in life."

Sue nods, "Okay. I get that."

I expand, "Anyone can call him God, and pray to him, but those who become his children by faith get to call him 'Father.' The word Jesus uses to pray is 'Abba.' It means 'Daddy.'"

"Wow. That's so beautiful." Sue is very expressive.

"Jesus became a man so that we could become children of God. We have the same child-and-father status Jesus enjoys with God. One verse in the Bible says, 'Behold what manner of love the Father has given unto us, that we should be called children of God.' Someone else said the same thing another way, 'The Son of God became the Son of Man, so that the Sons of Men could become Sons of God.'"

Sue's eyes are shining. "That's so amazing. I'm so glad I can call God 'Father'."

After I leave, we continue to pray together over the phone. It's a few months later before we continue our conversation face to face. In the meantime, Sue is in the middle of her fight with cancer. She has had a mastectomy and is enduring chemo and radiation treatment. She has lost her hair.

We spend time catching up. I try to listen and engage my heart. I want to feel something of what she is going through. The topic turns to prayer. I ask Sue how her prayer life is going.

"Really good. I always call God 'Father' when I pray. It makes me feel close to God."

"Do you want to hear another cool thing you can pray?"

"Absolutely."

The second big thing about prayer is that when

you pray to God the Father you need to pray in Jesus' name." "Okay. Really? Tell me why."

I explain, "It has to do with God's nature. God is entirely love, but at the same time he is completely holy. He is absolutely perfect in everything he is, everything he says, and everything he does. God is holy in his love and he is loving in his holiness."

Sue takes a few seconds to think this over. "Yeah. I can see that. He has to be that way. Okay, how does that fit in with praying in Jesus' name?"

"Well it does, in a very important way. For one, you and I can't just wander into God's presence with our sins and failings. The Bible tells us, 'O Lord, your eyes are too holy to look upon evil.' We need forgiveness and healing and cleansing in order to be in the presence of God. We need to be holy in order to stand before a holy God."

"Are you saying we can't just pray and expect God to answer?"

"Right. But this is the good news, the very best news. This is what the good news of the gospel is all about. This is why Jesus came to earth. This is why he was willing to die."

Sue's eyes are wide open. So is her heart.

"When Jesus dies an amazing miracle happens. There is a great exchange. When he dies on the cross – he takes the sin of the world on his shoulders. When he dies he imparts his perfect righteousness to those who believe in him."

"How does that work?"

"Right. When we say, 'In Jesus' name' at the end of a prayer – we acknowledge it is only because of him that we can pray at all. Because of him we can call God Father. Because of him God accepts us as his holy children. This is the whole reason prayer is a 24/7 reality."

"Do I ever need that. I'm going to start praying in Jesus' name."

"It's not just a phrase. These words transform our prayer time completely. He carried our sins and sorrows on the cross and he carries us into the presence of God. Now we get to stay there forever. Like sons and daughters we have continual, uninterrupted intimate audience with God. I often picture myself like a little child, jumping up on his knee and just letting him hug me."

***

A few months later, Sue has come a long way. Her cancer is in remission. Her hair is growing back. Considering the tough time she has been through – Sue is doing great.

She also finds a vibrant church and meets new friends that embrace her. Sue gets to know the pastor and his wife and goes to their home group. She tells me, "I just love going to church. It brings meaning and joy into my life." Her daughter Taylor gets lots out of it too. Her husband tries for a while, but is not really interested. Still, it seems the tide has turned for the good.

Then it happens. Another bomb drops. After 17 years together, after sharing this terrible battle with cancer, her husband tells her he wants to leave the marriage. Sue is leveled.

They try counseling. It doesn't take root. After months of anguish and empty hopes, Sue realizes it's over.

Over the phone we talk and pray together. The confusion, the anger, the tears come pouring out. She tells me this breakup is harder than fighting cancer. She is deeply shaken. Still, she takes her hurts to God and shares them openly with those who love her. They come alongside. Her friends at church pray with her. We continue our brother-sister relationship over the phone. I try to help. I've never felt more of a brother than now.

***

One day she asks the obvious question. "John, maybe you can help me. How come I get to know God, I start to follow him, and then everything falls apart? I just don't get it."

As I listen I try to understand. Hurt doesn't describe what she is going through.

I want to help, "Susan, I wonder if there might be a different way to look at it." She looks at me with questions in her eyes.

"I know you've had a lot of hard things happen Sue. You have a lot of tears, but you have a lot of courage too."

"I don't feel very courageous."

"I know. But let me ask, don't you think God knew ahead of time what you would be going through? Doesn't it make sense that He met you, made you his special child, so that he could carry you through all these troubles?"

"I want to believe that."

"He's a big God. Nothing is beyond his care for you. None of this has taken him by surprise."

"Yeah. That has to be right."

"I'm sure that's what's going on. Far from abandoning you to the trials, God has come to you at just the right time – just when he knows you most need him. He loves you so much he has come into your heart and life when you can't possibly face these troubles without him." "That makes sense. It still hurts, but it helps."

***

Summer comes round again. It's been another long year for Sue. It's also a year or so since we started our prayer talks. It's another sunny day at the cottage. We're sitting in the same corner as before. After catching up, we get around to a third prayer lesson.

"How is your prayer life coming along Sue?" "Really great, John. Every time I pray I call God Father. I end my prayers saying 'in Jesus' name.'"

"Terrific. How does that make you feel?"

She thinks for a minute. "You know what? I enjoy praying more and more. When I'm filled with anxiety, I pray to God and he gives me peace. I know I can talk to my father about anything. I know that because Jesus died for me, I can come to God any time and he hears my prayers."

"Sue, you're growing by leaps and bounds. You can't believe how much you're encouraging me."

She beams.

"I know about a third important lesson of prayer? Are you interested?"

"Of course I am. Go for it."

"Here it is. Every day I always ask God to fill me with his Holy Spirit."

"Okay. What does that mean? I didn't know I should do that."

"We need at least three things from God in order to live life with joy and hope. First we need to know God as our Father. Second, we need forgiveness through Jesus. We talked about that. One more thing – the third thing – we also need healing and the power to live life like sons and daughters of God. None of us has the strength and power to live this life on our own."

"Okay. So this is important. How do we get that?"

"Power for life is all about asking each day for the Holy Spirit to fill us. The Spirit brings us into the healing joy and power of Christ."

I use an illustration, "In the book of Revelation chapter 22, you can read about a great river that flows from God's throne and from the presence of Christ." Sue asks, "What does the river do?"

"Well, like any river, it brings water for replenishing. There are trees on either side of the river. They bear fruit every month of the year. This river provides drinking water. It provides water for cleansing. Those who immerse in this water find healing and new life. This river is a picture of the Holy Spirit. When Jesus ascended to heaven he poured out his Holy Spirit like a river into the hearts of every believer. Like a great and deep stream, the Holy Spirit brings healing and refreshment to our souls. The Holy Spirit is the source of all of our power for living."

Sue takes a minute to respond. "I never thought of it that way. So is that why we get the Holy Spirit when we believe?"

"Right. Jesus says, 'I stand at the door and knock, if anyone hears and opens, my father and I will come in and make our home with him.' Not only do we get to be in God's presence but God will come to live right in our hearts. The very minute someone trusts in Christ and opens the door, the Holy Spirit comes to live within them. Every true believer has the Spirit of Christ, the Holy Spirit living within."

"Okay, but tell me something. If we have the Holy Spirit within us, why do we have to ask for more each day?"

"Good question. It's about replenishing. We are given the Holy Spirit when we believe, but we are also invited to be filled with the Holy Spirit. Jesus encourages us to pray for the Holy Spirit before anything else. Filling is a matter of degree. We can be more or less filled. God won't leave us but the tank can run dry. Jesus promises, 'Much more will your heavenly father give the Holy Spirit to those who ask.' Another passage says, 'always be filled with the Holy Spirit.' Jesus wants us to ask for the Holy Spirit every day and he promises to fill us each time."

"Okay. I think I get it. I understand. If I want everything God has to give me I have to pray three things. I need to call God 'Father.' I pray 'in Jesus name." Third, I am going to ask God to fill me with his Spirit. "

I smile. She smiles. "Amen!"

Sue is still praying these three things.

LEAD US NOT INTO TEMPTATION BUT DELIVER US FROM EVIL

Chapter 11 from God in the Conversation

Pilgrim's Progress by John Bunyan is one of the most popular parables in the English language. The main character, Christian, is on a pilgrimage from the City of Destruction to the Celestial City.

He faces seen and unseen foes. He falls into the Slough of Despond, spends time in Doubting Castle and is tempted by sensual pleasure and ambition in the city Vanity Fair. In a crucial battle, he goes head to head with Apollyon, (another name for Satan) who is the malevolent "ruler of this world." Christian defends himself with the shield of faith and the sword of truth. He is guarded by "All Prayer" – the comprehensive defense and weapon of faith.

Bunyan's imagery is close to the Biblical language and metaphor. The Christian life is a war within a journey. We need prayer for the battle. We need prayer for the journey – each and every day. When we pray, "Lead us not into temptation, but deliver us from evil," we are asking for at least four things. First, we ask for God to lead us. Second, we pray for eyes of faith. Third, we ask God to defend us from temptations and trials. Fourth, we ask for God's guiding presence and power.

1. In this journey we ask for God to lead us

When we pray "lead us not into temptation," we are implicitly asking our heavenly father to be our guide and companion through the journey and battles of life until, safe at last, we come home to his heavenly kingdom.

God taught the lesson of his leading to the Israelites as they journeyed for forty years through the wilderness. He went before them in a pillar of cloud by day and a pillar of fire by night. The pillar is a picture of the Holy Spirit. Being led by that Spirit is a summary of the Christian journey:

Those who are led by the Spirit of God are sons of God. (Romans 8:14)

When we pray "lead us not into temptation," we acknowledge that life's path is often hard and painful. "Temptation" is used in its original sense, to mean trial and testing. When we ask God to lead us, we are praying that he will give us grace to face, courage to endure, and power to overcome that kind of temptation.

Jesus provides the perfect example of following his heavenly father when he faces trial and testing in the Garden of Gethsemane:

Going a little farther, he fell with his face to the ground and prayed, "My Father, if it is possible, may this cup be taken from me. Yet not as I will, but as you will." (Matthew 26:39)

Jesus is asking, if possible, to be led away from the last temptation – dying on a cross. At the same time he is praying for grace to accept God's leading and for courage to endure it.

We share our prayer with Jesus when we pray, "Lead us not into temptation." We experience suffering and loss. We endure. Following him, we come through to victory.

2. To advance, we need to see the whole picture

Albert Einstein was perhaps the greatest genius of the twentieth century. When he devised the theories of special and general relativity, it was assumed that he discovered the key to understanding the universe. However, as late as 1924 Einstein and everyone else thought that the Milky Way constituted the universe. Now we know that there are as many as 100 billion other galaxies in the universe – each with more than 100 billion stars! Einstein "saw" only a small part of the picture.

In much the same way, the world before our eyes is only a small part of life. We should invite new discovery, welcome new paradigms and not hold tightly to a safe and familiar picture. We can continue to explore and enjoy the universe we see, but be open to a far greater reality of which this seen world is only a part.

Where does prayer fit in this? Prayer is like a spiritual Hubble telescope, lifting us far above the earth's perspective to see the entire cosmos like God sees it. As we pray, glimpses of invisible galaxies come into view.

This directly relates to our request, "Lead us not into temptation." Because God creates everything visible and invisible, these two "halves" of existence are deeply related and in constant interplay. Forces of good and evil are in constant conflict.

This is the Christian worldview. Every person, community, church, and Christian is engaged in a very real battle against temptation, guilt, and despair. The instrument of attack can be other people, social forces, media, unseen personalities, or simply one's own unbelief and self-doubt.

This fight matters. If we quit and give in there will be no victory. Yet ultimately, in the final hour, Jesus himself will physically appear with his angels and defeat all of his and our enemies.

Be self-controlled and alert. Your enemy the devil prowls around like a roaring lion looking for someone to devour. Resist him, standing firm in the faith, because you know that your brothers throughout the world are undergoing the same kind of sufferings. And the God of all grace, who called you to his eternal glory in Christ, after you have suffered a little while, will himself restore you and make you strong, firm and steadfast. To him be the power for ever and ever. Amen. (1 Peter 5:8-11)

Prayer connects us to the power and presence of Jesus, our coming King. As we pray in expectation, his resurrection life flows into our hearts by the Holy Spirit he gives us. He enables us to defend against every seen and unseen enemy, and to advance in his promised victory.

3. We pray to overcome temptation

In this visible/invisible battle we fight different varieties of temptation on different fronts. There are at least four battle lines where temptation occurs.

First, we are tempted through the weakness of our fallen nature. Inordinate desire, deviant passion, envy and avarice, arrogance, hatred, and pride are within each of us. As Dorothy Sayers calls it, this "interior dislocation of the soul" accounts for much of the bloodshed, brokenness, and betrayal found in the human story. Our own inner compulsion (not God or the devil) leads us into every temptation:

When tempted, no one should say, "God is tempting me." For God cannot be tempted by evil, nor does he tempt anyone; but each one is tempted when, by his own evil desire, he is dragged away and enticed. Then, after desire has conceived, it gives birth to sin; and sin, when it is full grown, gives birth to death. (James 1:13-15)

Second, temptation surrounds us. As pollution clogs the air of the cities of the world, so we live in an atmosphere of temptation. We need prayer to breathe the fresh air of heaven. And we need it in special measure in a world where media has made the lure of temptation far more potent. For example, sexual exploitation and predation are fueled by "sexy" magazine covers, promiscuous sitcoms, salacious talk shows, and seductive advertising. Through the Internet, base passions are excited in increasing frequency and intensity.

Little is being done to slow the avalanche. We reserve moral outrage for those who would try to restrict our access to this "information." One person noted, "Even to avoid evil makes one a marked man." We pray fervently to withstand temptation because we are constantly surrounded by it.

Third, moral and spiritual assault comes in the form of false teaching. Take the popular adventure novel *The Da Vince Code*, which represents Jesus as a pagan leader who participated in ritual sex and sired children through Mary Magdalene. Though none of the alleged documents the author uses to support his argument have ever been discovered, he represents this lie as history.

Because so few know the Bible's portrait of Jesus, enormous numbers are drawn in and are dead serious about his viewpoints. (*Breaking the Da Vinci Code* by Peter Jones is a good antidote.) The Bible warns that in every age, new "Christs" will arise. The objective of these "antichrists" is to mislead believers and to prevent others from getting to know who Jesus really is:

Jesus answered: "Watch out that no one deceives you. For many will come in my name, claiming, 'I am the Christ,' and will deceive many." (Matthew 24:4,5)

When we pray, "Lead us not into temptation," we pray for faith to resist false teachings about Christ.

Fourth, the trials, sufferings and betrayals of life tempt us to question or even abandon our faith in God. It is really this doubting of God which is at the root of every temptation.

Our spiritual life is like a ship. Faith is the hull. In naval warfare, if the hull is strong and holds, little significant damage results from a cannon attack. Only if cannon balls pierce the hull is there penetration to the heart of the vessel.

In the same way, every assault of evil is first directed at this hull – our faith. Using accusation, trial, and temptation, Satan wants to wreck our connection to God and for us to question his goodness, power, and love. If he succeeds – the hull is breached and we begin to sink. Once we doubt the goodness, grace and power of God we are immediately vulnerable.

On our own we are outgunned and outmanned by a superior enemy. But as we pray, Jesus strengthens and comforts us in temptation: "I have prayed that your faith might stand." The apostle Paul encourages us:

God will not permit you to be tempted beyond what you are able to endure but when you are tempted he will also provide a way out that you may be able to withstand it. (1 Corinthians 10:13)

Paul is not saying that we will never fall into sin. What he means is that though we will be tempted and sometimes fail, by his grace and power we will grow in faith and live to fight another day.

As we ask God not to lead us into temptation our greatest encouragement is Jesus himself. He endured every temptation Satan could throw at him (Luke 4:1-13). One reason he did all this is so that he would be able to defend and protect us against every temptation we face:

Because he himself suffered when he was tempted, he is able to help those who are being tempted. (Hebrews 2:18)

4. God's presence and power: how God's kingdom advances

This prayer moves from defense, "Lead us not into temptation," to advance, "Deliver us from evil." Ultimately we not only survive the battles of life, we win. The reason for this is Jesus. His victory over sin and death at the cross and empty tomb is decisive and complete. The present age is a brief moment of history and the final "wrap up" is soon coming.

It is like the end of World War II. The decisive battle for the Allied victory is fought at Normandy. After this battle it is only one year before complete surrender and the signing of treaties.

In prayer, by faith, a believer appropriates and participates in Jesus' victory in every spiritual and practical area of this life. The victory we share with Jesus is seen and unseen, practical and spiritual.

For example, we work with a local ministry for sexually exploited women and their children called Genesis Vancouver. When we pray for a sexually exploited woman to be delivered, we desire her to experience the grace of forgiveness and spiritual healing. We also ask for her to be delivered from the pimps, johns and abusive people who prey on her and use her as a slave. Anything less would be less than Jesus intends:

This is part of the prayer for the Kingdom: it is the prayer that the forces of destruction, of dehumanization, of anti-creation, of anti-redemption may be bound and gagged, and that God's good world may escape from being sucked down into their morass. ~NT Wright

As John Wesley said, "There is no Christianity that is not a social Christianity." When we pray, "Deliver us from evil," we include social justice and mercy:

What does the Lord require of you, O man, but to do justice, and to love mercy and to walk humbly with your God? (Micah 6:8)

Prayer is the key to victory in all spiritual warfare. Karl Barth writes, "When God's people clasp their hands in prayer, it is the beginning of an uprising against the disorder of the world."

When we pray, God will give us courage for each day's battle – and also promises to act:

For he will deliver the needy who cry out, the afflicted who have no one to help. He will take pity on the weak and the needy and save the needy from death. He will rescue them from oppression and violence, for precious is their blood in his sight. (Psalm 72:12-14)

Bring it Home

Pray It Forward

- Personal prayer at home:

  Write out your experiences with God this week.

  What are some of the scriptures that moved you?

  Think about your friendship with Christ in prayer.

  • Pray through the Prayer Evangelism cycle. Pray for the opportunity to offer to teach your friend(s) how to pray.

     1. Pray for appointments.
     2. Pray *for* someone.
     3. Pray *with* someone. Invite them to offer up a prayer.
     4. Offer to teach them to pray.

Share It Outward

• **Prayer and practice steps with others:**

  1. Meet with two others (in person or by phone or online) to pray for these seeker friends.

  2. Build prayer friendships.

  By now you have deepened your prayer friendship with others. Hopefully you have had a chance to discuss their spiritual practices, and they have listened to you share yours, if you have been praying for them and also with them.

  In other words, if you are going deeper and they are drawn to listening to your story and asking questions, ask them if they would like to learn how to pray.

  Offer to meet with them.

  You can ask if they would like to read a book about Jesus' prayer (*Journey in Prayer with Jesus* is written and designed for seekers). Perhaps read a chapter or two at a time together, and you can meet to discuss the chapters. Be sure to pray together too.

Readings:

  • Read ahead and prepare Week 10.

WEEK TEN

Pray for Harvest Joy and Answers

Prayer is the greatest joy of the Christian life. Along the way, it is possible to lose the wonder of prayer. Somehow prayer becomes tedious and pedestrian, a formula of repeated phrases and words.

Sometimes, the problem is simply our sin. Sin makes us indifferent to God, which is why we end up indifferent to prayer.

Other times we lose the joy of prayer because we cease looking for answers. Jesus promises answers and joy to those who pray in his name.

We need to come to grips with the fullness of Jesus promise to hear and answer when we pray. Here are some of Jesus' astounding words:

> *If you ask me anything in my name, I will do it. (John 14:14)*
>
> *If you abide in me, and my words abide in you, ask whatever you wish, and it will be done for you. (John 15)*
>
> *I chose you and appointed you that you should go and bear fruit and that your fruit should abide, so that whatever you ask the Father in my name, he may give it to you.(John 15)*
>
> *Truly, truly, I say to you, whatever you ask of the Father in my name, he will give it to you. Until now you have asked nothing in my name. Ask, and you will receive, that your joy may be full. (John 16)*

Jesus gives us a lesson here: we should never be content to pray without receiving answers.

We all pray during trials and adversity. These prayers begin to be answered the minute they are prayed.

> *"At the beginning of your pleas for mercy a word went out...." (Daniel 9:23)*

<u>God's immediate answer to our prayer takes shape in four ways (at least):</u>

First, he will guard <u>you</u> through trial and give <u>you</u> endurance and patience

> *May you be strengthened with all power, according to his glorious might, for all endurance and patience with joy. Colossians 1:11 (see also James 1:2, 1 Peter 5:18, Psalm 119:67,71,75)*

Second, God lifts <u>you</u> above our trials so <u>you</u> rejoice in spite of them:

> *God will lift me high upon a rock. And now my head shall be lifted up above my enemies all around me, and I will offer in his tent sacrifices with shouts of joy; I will sing and make melody to the Lord. Psalm 27*

Third, he will deliver <u>you</u> from all evil at the right time- when <u>your</u> trials have worked his transforming purposes:

> *"Call upon me in the day of trial, I will deliver you and you will glorify me"*

Fourth and best of all, God reveals himself to us in midst of adversity:

> *Hear, O Lord, when I cry aloud; be gracious to me and answer me! You have said, "Seek my face." My heart says to you, "Your face, Lord, do I seek." (Psalm 27)*

As you seek God's face and his help, look for these answers during your trials. Be assured that God hears and answers your cry.

Jesus' promise to answer prayer is without limits- but not without guidelines.

We cannot ask selfishly

> *You ask and do not receive, because you ask wrongly, to spend it on your passions. James 4*

We need to be in fellowship- 'abide' with Christ to be answered:

> *If you abide in me, and my words abide in you, ask whatever you wish, and it will be done for you. John 15*

As we pray we need to believe he is willing and able to hear our prayer:

> *Therefore I tell you, whatever you ask in prayer, believe that you have received it, and it will be yours. Mark 11*

We break the promise when we refuse to obey him, especially when we bear a grudge against another:

> *Whatever you ask the Father in my name, he may give it to you. These things I command you, so that you will love one another. John 15*

Yes Jesus promises have guidelines. They do not limit his promise! Guidelines contain the promise- like the banks of a powerful river. Heavens storehouse is full and pregnant with waiting promises!

We can ask for anything if we ask in humble and joyful submission to Christ. Especially, we are encouraged to pray for the salvation of our friends, neighbors, relatives, and even those far off:

> *First of all, then, I urge that supplications, prayers, intercessions, and thanksgivings be made for all people...This is good, and it is pleasing in the sight of God our Savior, who desires all people to be saved and to come to the knowledge of the truth. 1 Tim 2:1ff*

Jesus answer will be harvest joy:

> *Already the one who reaps is receiving wages and gathering fruit for eternal life, so that sower and reaper may rejoice together. John 4:36*

Also:

> *I tell you, there will be more joy in heaven over one sinner who repents than over ninety-nine righteous persons who need no repentance. Luke 15*

Wrestle with Jesus as you wrestle with these prayer promises. He is powerful. He is faithful. He is willing. Ask for faith to believe and trust him to hear you. Pray to keep to his excellent guidelines. To grow in relationship with Jesus is to grow in prayer. To grow in prayer is to grow in the expectation and certainty of Jesus promise to answer.

Scripture Study

John 14:14 You may ask me for anything in my name, and I will do it.

John 15:7-8 If you remain in me and my words remain in you, ask whatever you wish, and it will be done for you. This is to my Father's glory, that you bear much fruit, showing yourselves to be my disciples.

Luke 15:7 I tell you that in the same way there will be more rejoicing in heaven over one sinner who repents than over ninety-nine righteous persons who do not need to repent.

After these 10 weeks of building prayer friendships, ponder, pray and write down answers to prayer in these areas:

Growth in your prayer friendship with Jesus

Growth in your prayer friendship in triads and this group

Growth in harvest joy – opportunities and conversions

Give thanks to God.

PRAYER PRACTICE:

Now each share your joy with the whole group. Praise God together in prayer.

Prayer Friendship Skill
EVALUATING PERSONAL PRAYER PROGRESS

Evaluate how you are growing in dynamic prayer friendship with Jesus and others (1=weak, 5=strong)

1 2 3 4 5   1. I am enjoying an intimate prayer friendship with Jesus
1 2 3 4 5   2. I personally experience growth in the grace and truth of the gospel in fresh ways
1 2 3 4 5   3. I am aware of my fears and obstacles to evangelism
1 2 3 4 5   4. I find power and confidence in Christ to share my faith with others
1 2 3 4 5   5. I feel a compassion and burden for the lost
1 2 3 4 5   6. I pray regularly for the salvation of lost friends
1 2 3 4 5   7. I team up to pray with other believers for the lost
1 2 3 4 5   8. I pray regularly for those who are marginalized and needy
1 2 3 4 5   9. I am getting to know people who are out of my circle of comfort
1 2 3 4 5   10. I get to know and pray for the deep heart/spiritual needs of people (not just practical needs)
1 2 3 4 5   11. I am alert and ready for divine appointments for God conversations with old and new people alike
1 2 3 4 5   12. I am practicing the kindness and hospitality of God towards those outside the faith
1 2 3 4 5   13. I spend time regularly with seeker friends
1 2 3 4 5   14. I have regular spiritual and God conversations with seekers
1 2 3 4 5   15. I am able to share Christ with seekers, bringing them to understand need for Christ's saving grace
1 2 3 4 5   16. I am able pray with seekers… bringing Christ into specific situations and needs of people
1 2 3 4 5   17. I regularly see answers to prayer as I pray for people
1 2 3 4 5   18. I see God using me to lead people to Christ
1 2 3 4 5   19. I am able to share my prayer/ personal experience with God
1 2 3 4 5   20. I am teaching non-Christians how to pray their way to Christ

Summarize where you are encouraged to see growth.

Summarize where you would like to trust God to strengthen you where you are weak.

PRAYER PRACTICE: Pray for each other to grow.

Readings

GOD IS IN CONVERSATION WITH EVERYONE

Conclusion from *God in the Conversation*

Whenever you talk with someone about God, God is in the conversation. I experience it all the time. God is not just the topic, he is a participant.

My aim in each of these God conversations is to hear God- often unexpectedly- and to help the other person hear him too. I encourage our Sikh taxi driver to make a connection between prayer in the temple and how God is able to inhabit the human heart. I ask Ivan the hitchhiker to consider that God might have a path to us in addition to our many paths to God. I challenge the school board leader to go within-- and to consider the seven deadly sins with which we all wrestle. I pray with Ted through his terminal cancer so he will find inner renewal from God as his body simply wastes away. As we pray together, we bring God into the conversation.

God wants us to find him.

The path to God is not so much about exploring a wilderness as it is about finding a path. Our quest for God follows the path that he has laid down. God gives us tracks to run on in our quest to find him. He leaves clues to his existence throughout the world and the universe. His kindness permeates life:

> *God has not left us without a witness, for he did good by giving you rains from heaven and fruitful seasons, satisfying your hearts with food and gladness... (Acts 14:17)*

When we stare up at the stars or see photos taken through the Hubble telescope, we see the might, splendor and genius of our Maker.

> *The heavens declare the glory of God,*
> *and the sky above proclaims his handiwork.*
> *Day to day pours out speech,*
> *and night to night reveals knowledge.*
> *There is no speech, nor are there words,*
> *whose voice is not heard.*
> *Their voice goes out through all the earth,*
> *and their words to the end of the world.*
> *(Psalm 19:1-4.)*

Quasars, pulsars, star-generating nebula, mind-numbing expanses, spiraling galaxies all remind us of an awesome God.

God is not creation, but he is present everywhere. In a mysterious way, God pervades every atom and electron. He is in the air we breathe and forms the environment in which we live:

> *In him we live and move and have our being. (Acts 17:28)*

God's consciousness fills the world.

> *Where can I flee from your presence?*
> *Wherever I turn you are there...(Psalm 139:7)*

The knowledge of God surrounds us and presses in upon us. Open your eyes to see. Tune your ears to hear. You are already on the path to God.

Even as we 'discover' God, a previous awareness of God comes to the surface.

I recall meeting relatives from Denmark. My parents were immigrants. I was born in Canada so I did not grow up around my relatives. Still when I would meet an aunt, uncle or cousin, it was as if I was meeting someone I already knew. Our shared history came to the surface. There was immediate recognition and sense of kinship.

The first time I prayed to God I had a similar sense of deja vu. I was a troubled teen, wrestling with life. I worked for my father's furniture making company. I went to install some cabinets at a convent. During the lunch break I strolled up to the garden. It was lush with flowering bushes. A path wound through it. Every so often, along the path, there was a station with a statue – Mary, Jesus, a cross, or one of the saints. As I walked the pathway I stopped here and there to relax. I could "feel" the setting.

A strange thing happens. I sense something familiar. I feel at home somehow.

The flower-laden garden was restful. The pathway fit my need to "find a way." Everything, even the statues seemed to belong in this place. Somehow I belonged. It felt like home.

ENGAGE THE CONVERSATION with God, with believers, with seekers | WWW.PRAYERCURRENT.COM

I was invited into this setting. Somehow I knew "God is speaking to me. I am supposed to reply."

I got down on my knees and prayed, "God, I am not sure about you, but I want to know more. I want to believe in you. If you will help me find my way, and take this confusion and burden from me, I am yours."

I felt a wave of calm wash over me, from head to toe. My inner knot of angst was removed and peace filled my inmost being.

When I returned from work, I told my girlfriend, Caron (now my wife), "I met an old friend." Indeed I had. I met God.

God is out to get our attention

When I say that God is in the conversation, I mean he is active and engaged. God is out to get our attention. He is inviting a reply and seeking a dialogue.

In the New Testament we are told that God uses time and geography to encourage people to find him.

He himself gives to all mankind life and breath and everything. And he made from one man every nation of mankind to live on all the face of the earth, having determined allotted periods and the boundaries of their dwelling place, that they should seek God, and perhaps feel their way toward him and find him. Acts 17:25-27.

This is remarkable. Where we live and when we live is no accident. Our place and time are part of a greater plan for us to find God. In one sense, when it comes to finding God, we are all at the right place at the right time.

God awaits our reply

Because God is in conversation with each and every one of us, He awaits our reply. We can make sense of life. We can fulfill our purpose and destiny. But we have to engage in the conversation. This is what prayer is.

This is why I saved the prayer conversations for last. Praying with Karl, Susan and Ted is about opening the door to a direct conversation with God.

God is a prayer away.

If anyone hopes to find God, what a comfort to know that God wants to be found. A simple prayer is all that is needed:

You will seek me and you will find me when you seek me with all your heart.
(Jeremiah 29:7)

Seek the Lord while he may be found, call upon him while he is near.
(Isaiah 55:6)

They that seek me find me.
(Proverbs 8:17)

God is in the conversation. He is speaking to each and every one of us. When we pray it is our heart's reply.

Where To From Here?

Bring it Home

- **Pray it forward:**
    - How is Jesus asking me to follow him into the harvest field?
    - Begin to pray at 10:02am each day (see Luke 10:2.) Pray the Lord of the harvest to send forth laborers into his harvest.

- **Prayer and practice steps with others:**
    - Pray with your triad: pray for answers, celebrate advances in God' conversations and in praying with friends.
    - Pray to be able to bring others in until you can divide and multiply. When prayers are answered… celebrate!

    When someone comes to Christ, bring them into your triad.

    Begin to form another triad!

HOW TO STAY ENGAGED?

Continue the power of practicing regular prayer friendships in community and accountability. Watch God grow your harvest heart and give you open doors with seekers as you pray with others. Don't allow the momentum to fizzle due to busyness or isolation from like-minded mission-hearted believers. Be on guard against the enemy who seeks to destroy the seeds planted here.

SOME PRAYER EVANGELISM IDEAS:

- Take more prayer evangelism **training**
- Start praying **intentionally** for seeker friends and open doors
- Prioritize and spend more **time** with seeker friends
- **Ask** my seeker friends how I can pray for them
- Find a prayer evangelism **accountability prayer** partner
- Read *God in the Conversation* for inspiration and guidance
- Host a prayer **book club outreach** *Journey in Prayer with Jesus*
- **Launch outreach** season with Prayer Evangelism **training**
- **Train Alpha/outreach** team in Prayer Evangelism

TAKE ACTION. How is God asking you respond?

PRAYER EVANGELISM ACTION POINTS:

Discerning through prayer and reflection, what are one or two prayer evangelism actions that you hear the Spirit stirring in you to do?

What are potential obstacles that might interfere with these? How might you counteract them in practical ways, in the power of the Spirit?

Commit your aims in prayer. Who will you share and pray with for accountability?